RUNNING STRONG & INJURY-FREE

JANET S. HAMILTON

Running Strong
191 Crossing Drive
Stockbridge, GA 30281

Cover and Book Design: Carol Buckle Design Illustration
Cover Photos: S & S Photography
Inside Photos: Harold Wood
Printing: B & B Print Source
Printed in the United States of America
First Printing — June 2001

Library of Congress Catalog Card Number 2001117669

Publisher's Cataloging in Publication

Hamilton, Janet S.
    Running strong & injury-free / Janet S. Hamilton.
    Includes bibliographical references and index.
    Preassigned LCCN: 2001117669.
    ISBN 0-9709611-0-3

TABLE OF CONTENTS

INTRODUCTION

Over the years I've been lucky enough to be involved with the training of many devoted athletes of all shapes, sizes and abilities. Watching and helping these athletes come back from injuries that could have been avoided with a few preventative measures made me realize that armed with a little knowledge these athletes may have avoided a great many of these. Encouraged by friends, I decided to put together this book – covering the basics of injury prevention. What follows is based on current research, as well as my personal experience of over twenty years of helping athletes of all ages and abilities back to their chosen sport. Information presented is by no means exhaustive, and will continue to develop over time as new research sheds light on the ever-changing field of human performance.

Let me emphasize right off the bat—*this book is not intended to substitute in any way for sound medical advice.* It is intended to help athletes understand some of the possible factors involved in injuries. By understanding these factors and following the principles of smart training it is hoped that injuries will be avoided. *If you're injured, seek the advice and care of trained medical professionals* – doctors, physical therapists, podiatrists and chiropractors can offer important insight into your current injury, your past injury pattern and guide you in your rehabilitation process. Nothing can substitute for the skilled hands of a physical therapist, the diagnostic skills of a physician, or the observant eyes and knowledge of a good coach. **Exercises presented in this book are not intended to substitute for clinical rehabilitation of injured athletes.** Check with your medical professional if you're injured, and see which (if any) of the exercises are appropriate for you. Never delay in seeking medical advice because of something you've read here (or anywhere else for that matter).

While this book is directed principally to runners and walkers, all persons, athlete or not, will benefit from information and instructions concerning strength and flexibility. Like most aspects of life, achieving a balance is the goal. It's easier if you're aware of the factors involved and are operating from a broad foundation of understanding. If this book broadens your knowledge of how to avoid injuries while pursuing your activity of choice, it will have achieved its goal.

On to the basics—

BASIC PRINCIPLES

The first step to preventing a running injury is to understand some of the factors that contribute to them. Numerous studies have attempted to figure out why and how runners get injured. All have come up with a fairly consistent picture – there is no one reason why runners get injured, but there is a pretty consistent interaction of factors that play a role in most runner injuries. Factors commonly recognized include muscle weakness, inadequate flexibility, training errors, poor or incorrect running shoes and poor or abnormal biomechanics. Biomechanics, for our purposes at least, can best be defined as the sequence of events that occur when the foot hits the ground. There is an intricate chain of events that take place with each foot strike, including actions and reactions at each joint from your toes all the way up your spine. What happens when the foot hits the ground is at least partly determined by your skeletal alignment…how your body lines up. This is largely determined by your genetics, so make sure to pick your parents carefully! Each of the above mentioned factors (flexibility, strength, biomechanics and training) appear to have an individual contribution to injury patterns, and can also have an effect on each of the other factors. It can get a little confusing, so it helps to draw a picture to illustrate these interactions.

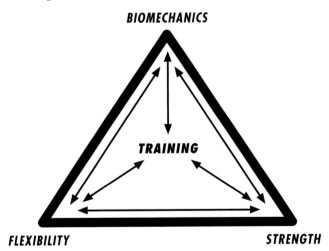

For instance, muscle flexibility can be affected by an individual's biomechanics and likewise, an individual's biomechanics can be affected by muscle flexibility. A prime example of this is the increase in pronation that takes place as a direct result of loss of flexibility in the calf muscle group. The tighter those calf muscles get, the more the foot seems to pronate! Conversely, people who pronate excessively often have very tight calf muscles. Muscle strength and flexibility also interact with each other. Training errors (like adding too much mileage too fast, or doing too much speedwork) can contribute to micro-trauma and a loss of flexibility as well as to a loss of strength and a deterioration of biomechanics. With this picture in mind, it is no surprise that research into injury prevention is on-going and sometimes produces confusing results. It is difficult to control all the various factors so that one factor at a time can be studied. It seems clear though that to avoid injury you must deal with as many variables as possible. We'll cover each of the factors attributed to running injuries in turn, starting with a basic understanding of the biomechanics of running.

CHAPTER ONE

UNDERSTANDING THE BIOMECHANICS OF GAIT

The sequence of events that occur when your foot hits the ground affects everything from your toes up. How your body responds to the stress of running or walking and how it absorbs shock and adapts to uneven terrain sets the stage for all that follows. This is really about what happens "when the rubber hits the road". To understand this, a brief anatomy lesson is warranted. Your foot is made up of 26 bones (28 if you count the two little sesamoid bones), linked together in an intricate fashion so that it can perform two very different jobs. One job is to absorb shock and adapt to uneven terrain, the other is to become a rigid lever so that you can push off and take a step. Shock absorption and adaptation to uneven terrain require <u>mobility</u>, whereas propulsion requires <u>stability.</u> In order to accomplish these two very different tasks, your foot goes through motions that incorporate three planes of movement at once. (Think back to high school geometry...the x, y and z-axes) These combined, tri-planar motions are called pronation and supination. The motion of pronation "unlocks" the foot so that it can absorb shock and adapt. Supination on the other hand is a relative "locking" of the foot so that it can propel you forward. These motions are absolutely indispensable for optimum gait. So, for those of you who thought pronation was a bad thing, or a disease of some type, relax. Pronation is a good thing...at the right time and to the right degree. In fact, a foot that doesn't pronate enough (sometimes known as "pes cavus") can also cause problems; though using a more cushioned shoe can often compensate for this. Let's get a look at pronation on some real feet.

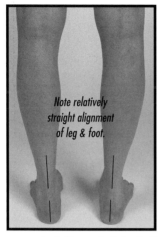

Note relatively straight alignment of leg & foot.

What does pronation really look like?

The picture to the left shows a neutral alignment of the foot and the lower leg. From behind, it appears that if you were to draw a line bisecting the heel bone (calcaneus) and the lower third of the leg, the lines would intersect in a fairly straight-line fashion and this represents what the alignment of the foot and lower leg ideally should look like in a static stance position. The picture to the right shows feet that are excessively

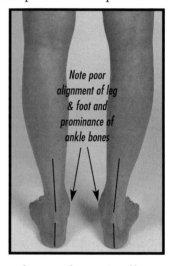

Note poor alignment of leg & foot and prominance of ankle bones

pronated. From behind, the two lines bisecting the calcaneus and lower leg no longer line up straight. Because the feet are connected to the tibia (lower leg bone) and the tibia is connected to the femur (thigh bone), this motion is transmitted up the kinetic chain and places a greater stress on the muscles, tendons, ligaments and joints of the feet, lower leg, knee, hip and lower back. What happens at one end of the kinetic chain can have a dramatic effect on the other end of the kinetic chain. It gives the term "chain reaction" a whole new meaning. The bigger perspective, looking from the hips down, demonstrates the effect of pronation on the entire leg. The photo to the left shows a neutral alignment of the feet, resulting in nice, straight alignment of the entire leg. The photo to the right shows the same individual in relaxed stance. The excessive pronation affects the alignment of the entire leg. Things just don't look as straight anymore. The lines at her ankle,

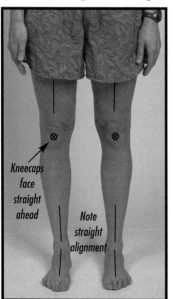

Kneecaps face straight ahead

Note straight alignment

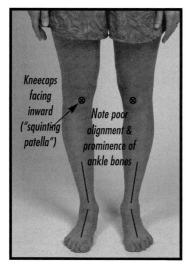

Kneecaps facing inward ("squinting patella")

Note poor alignment & prominence of ankle bones

which appear relatively straight on the left, intersect at an angle in relaxed stance on the right. Notice too that her kneecaps appear to be looking straight ahead in the picture on the left, whereas on the right they appear to be looking more toward one another (believe it or not, this is referred to as "squinting patella"). These photos only show one piece of the puzzle though, static stance. Walking and running aren't the same as static stance so we have to consider what position the foot should be in at each point of the gait cycle from initial contact to push off.

PHASES OF THE GAIT CYCLE

Initial contact

Between 75% and 90% of runners contact the ground heel first[5]. However, a smaller percentage contacts the ground initially with the mid-foot or even forefoot region of the foot. Initially it was surmised that the faster you're running the further forward toward the midfoot or forefoot the initial contact will be, however recent research seems to show that the initial contact point remains relatively constant for a given individual running at different speeds[5]. At heel strike, the foot should be slightly inverted or "supinated". In this position, the initial contact is usually slightly to the lateral (outer side) of a point directly at the back of the heel bone. When you look at the wear pattern on your shoes, you may notice that the outer side of the heel is more worn than the inner side of the heel. Some people erroneously infer from this that they are "under pronators" or "supinators" when in fact this is usually not the case. This wear pattern is completely normal. This initial contact position of slight supination is a stable; relatively "locked" position from which the foot then rapidly pronates or "unlocks" to come into full contact with the ground[14]. As the foot and leg pronate, the muscles that control this motion begin the process of absorbing body weight and ground reaction forces. Some of the primary muscles responsible for this include muscles of the thigh and buttock in addition to the muscles of the lower leg. The thigh and buttock muscles control the flexion (bending) that occurs at the knee joint and act as primary shock absorbers in the kinetic chain. The rapid pronation of the foot that occurs right after heel strike sets these actions in motion. Without the right amount of pronation after initial contact, the ability to absorb shock is impaired. Interestingly, it was initially presumed that the greatest amount of force on the foot would be borne by the heel bone shortly after contact, but it has been subsequently found that the greatest amount of vertical force occurs later in the stance phase when the weight is primarily on the forefoot region[3]. It appears that the excessive wear on the lateral heel region of a running or walking shoe is not the result of compressive force so much as it is the result of shear forces occurring at the moment of contact.

Midstance

This phase of gait encompasses the period from full foot contact (which occurs at the end of the initial contact phase) through the weight-bearing phase until the heel begins to lift off the ground. Pronation, which started at heel contact (as described above), continues until the early midstance phase, when the foot should stop pronating and begin to re-supinate in preparation for push off. This marks a significant transition from the role of "shock absorber" to the role of "stable platform". A normal foot position during the middle part of midstance phase is neutral to very slightly pronated; however the pronation motion of the foot has stopped and the foot is now moving toward a more supinated position[6]. It is moving in that direction but isn't there yet. That is for the next phase of gait.

Late stance and push off

This phase begins as the body weight shifts more to the forefoot region and the heel begins to elevate off the ground. At this point the foot should be re-supinated at least to neutral so that it can "lock" the bones into a stable and more rigid lever for push off. If the foot remains pronated in this later phase of gait, it is relatively "unlocked" and you're essentially trying to propel yourself off of a somewhat unstable surface. The bones of the forefoot are not positioned optimally to accept the large force being generated. The importance of "locking" the foot shouldn't be underestimated. For example, if you're walking in soft sand you'll find it takes significantly more effort to cover a distance than if you are walking on firm terrain. This is a graphic example of what happens when there is no rigid surface from which to push off. The effort required to take a step is greatly increased. A foot that stays pronated into the late stance or push off phase is inefficient – like walking on soft sand.

➲ *A foot that stays pronated into the late stance or push off phase is inefficient – like walking on soft sand.*

Remember that the greatest loads on the foot occur during this late-stance phase of gait. Compounding these loads by having an unstable platform due to excessive pronation can greatly increase the risk of injury.

Swing phase

This is the non-weight-bearing phase of gait as the leg is swinging forward to take the next step. The hamstring muscles and the gluteal muscles decelerate the forward momentum of the leg just before the foot contacts the ground. Though injury rarely occurs during this phase of gait, strains of these muscles can occur very shortly after contact as a result of their high level of activity in decelerating this forward momentum.

NOW I UNDERSTAND IT, WHAT CAN I DO ABOUT IT?

Should I try to "fix" my gait? Generally speaking this is a lousy idea. Unless you have acquired a habitual limp due to a traumatic injury like an ankle sprain, it is rarely recommend that you try to consciously change the way you run or walk. Pronation and supination are complex tri-planar motions that occur in less than six tenths of a second when walking and less than 2 tenths of a second when running[6]. It is hard to think that fast. Assuming that you could think that fast, you would be focusing on one part of the gait pattern and quite likely would "fix" one problem and simultaneously cause ten others in the process. It is just not worth it. You run or walk the way you do because of a complex interaction between your skeletal alignment (genetics), your flexibility, your strength, your terrain, your footwear and numerous other variables. You can indirectly affect the way you walk or run by changing some of these variables, like flexibility or strength or shoes or terrain, but trying to directly (consciously) alter your gait pattern will probably not achieve the results you wanted.

> ● Pronation and supination are complex tri-planar motions that occur in less than six tenths of a second when walking and less than 2 tenths of a second when running[6]. It is hard to think that fast. Assuming that you could think that fast, you would be focusing on one part of the gait pattern and quite likely would "fix" one problem and simultaneously cause ten others in the process.

Terrain

Changing to a softer terrain, though intuitively a good choice for injured athletes, is often the wrong choice. If the injury is related to excessive or late pronation, training on a very soft surface like a bark-chip path or sand will take away some of the inherent stability offered by firmer terrain like a packed dirt path or rubberized running track. Without a stable platform, the foot will pronate further and longer and the strain on the muscles, tendons and bony tissues will increase dramatically. If the injury is the result of inadequate shock absorption due to a lack of adequate pronation (pes cavus) then switching to a slightly softer surface like dirt or a bark chip path may help. Altering the training route to a more level surface may alleviate some of the stress imparted by uneven surfaces or hilly terrain. For most injured athletes a rubberized track or packed dirt path that is fairly level offers the best of both worlds – stability and shock absorption. Changing terrain from day to day can help avoid injury by building strength. Always running or walking on the same side of the road or on the same surface can contribute to overuse injuries. Throw a little variety in your week.

Shoes

Although it may seem sensible to buy walking shoes if you're walking and running shoes if you're running, at this point walking shoes just haven't come as far in their development as running shoes. Most walkers will do best to purchase running shoes rather than walking shoes for their training. A huge amount of research has gone into the construction of the ideal running shoe. Since their introduction in 1865, major improvements in materials and technology have dramatically improved the characteristics of running shoes[5]. One clear fact remains though; there is no ONE perfect shoe. The characteristics of the shoe need to match the characteristics of your foot.

Shoes can be thought of as existing along a continuum from very stable to very flexible. The more stable the shoe, generally the less cushioned it will be and conversely the more cushioned the shoe the less stability it offers. Changing to a different shoe can sometimes hold the key to alleviating injury. The trick is to know something about your particular biomechanical gait pattern

> ➲ *If you're plagued with injuries, it may be worth your time and effort to see a specialist who can evaluate your gait pattern and point you in the right direction. Some of the professionals who may be able to help you include orthopedists who specialize in sports injuries or foot and ankle injuries, podiatrists, physical therapists who specialize in orthopedics or sports injuries, exercise physiologists who specialize in biomechanics, or even a seasoned running coach who has taken the time to learn the intricacies of the human gait pattern.*

so that you make informed decisions when purchasing running shoes. This can sometimes pose a challenge, as most of us can't see ourselves run. If your particular biomechanics call for stability due to excessive amounts or late timing of pronation then buying a shoe with top notch cushioning will probably contribute to injury or make existing injuries worse. On the other hand, if you have a rigid, high arched foot (pes cavus) then buying a shoe with top notch cushioning may be just what you need. If you're plagued with injuries, it may be worth your time and effort to see a specialist who can evaluate your gait pattern and point you in the right direction. Some of the professionals who may be able to help you include orthopedists who specialize in sports injuries or foot and ankle injuries, podiatrists, physical therapists who specialize in orthopedics or sports injuries, exercise physiologists who specialize in biomechanics, or even a seasoned running coach who has taken the time to learn the intricacies of the human gait pattern. Use of a treadmill and video camera can greatly enhance the accuracy of the analysis, as catching the more subtle movements in "real time" is often difficult (remember, the "fun stuff" happens in less than .6 seconds when walking and less than .2 seconds when running). Close working relationships between these skilled professionals and the experienced technicians at a running shoe store can make the shoe selection process easier. The practitioner who evaluates your gait pattern will be able to guide you to a particular type of shoe, for example one with more cushioning or more stability. The skilled technician at the shoe store will be able to show you several different models from different manufacturers that offer the characteristics your practitioner has determined that you need. If you don't have a technical running shoe store in your area, then reading the shoe reviews offered in popular running magazines is a good place to start when investigating various shoe characteristics since running shoe manufacturers tend to make subtle (and sometimes not so subtle) changes to their shoes fairly frequently. Talking to other runners and asking questions of the staff at the shoe store also offers insight into what shoes have worked well for other runners with your particular foot type.

Shoe "lasts"

The shape of the shoe, known as the "last", can play a role in the motion control characteristics of the shoe and is also a crucial part of how the shoe feels on your foot. The last you need will be partly determined by the shape of your foot and also by the motion control or cushioning characteristics that you need. Generally speaking, the more curved the last of the shoe, the less motion control it will offer. Conversely the straighter the last, generally the stronger the shoe is in the motion control department. Shoe manufacturers have lots of other tricks to give the shoe different characteristics of control or cushioning. One way to accomplish this is to use different density materials within the midsole, with the more dense material usually being on the inner side to help control pronation. Use of special foot beds, different configurations of leather stitching on the upper, and different shock absorbing materials in the midsole, like air or gel pockets are some other ways they can manipulate the characteristics of the shoe. The manufacturers are always looking for new and better ways to deal with the needs of runners and walkers, so materials and construction change frequently.

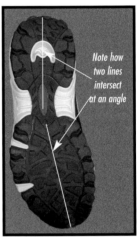

The first two photos show shoes constructed from a fairly straight last. This type of shoe is often marketed as a motion-controlling shoe. The right photo shows a shoe that is semi curved and has flex grooves in the midsole to enhance its flexibility and cushioning characteristics.

Life expectancy

Replacing worn shoes is crucial to injury prevention and recovery. A worn shoe will no longer have the strength to control motion, or the elasticity to rebound and absorb shock. The deterioration of these characteristics is subtle and often goes unnoticed until an injury occurs. Be pro-active in this regard and replace your shoes before they become excessively worn. Recent publications have indicated that running shoes need to be replaced every 300-400 training miles [1,2]. When you're training at marathon intensity of 40 miles a week or more that translates to a new pair of shoes about every 7 to 10 weeks.

If the shoe fits...

Fitting the shoe correctly to your foot is another area of concern. When trying on shoes, wear the socks you usually use for training and if you wear custom orthotics, or over-the-counter arch supports take them with you. It is important to get shoes that will work well with your existing supports, and have adequate room to accommodate the devices. To insure adequate room in the toe box of the shoe, you should allow about a half an inch of space between the end of your longest toe and the end of the toe box when your foot is fully weighted. For many runners, this can mean the difference between healthy toenails and no toenails after a long downhill run.

Lace it up!

Lace your shoes snug to your foot to optimize the motion control capability of the shoe. Depending on your foot structure, different lacing systems may make the shoe fit more comfortably over bony prominences or keep your heel from slipping in and out of the heel counter of the shoe. By finding a comfortable lacing system you'll be able to tie the shoe more snugly to your foot and insure that the upper and midsole of the shoe offer optimum performance.

For narrow heels

To avoid heel slippage try this "loop" system of lacing. Simply lace the shoe as you usually would, then at the next to the last eyelet at the top of the shoe thread the lace back through the top eyelet on the same side rather than crossing it to the other side of the shoe. This creates a loop. Place the lace from the right side through the left loop and the lace from the left side through the right loop. "See-saw" the laces back and forth to

Make a loop here by bringing lace up through this hole then back through the top hole

Then bring other lace through loop

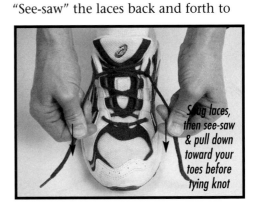

Snug laces, then see-saw & pull down toward your toes before tying knot

pull the loops snug against the shoe, then pull the laces down toward your toe before tying your shoe. This downward tug of the laces will help pull the heel counter of the shoe more snugly against your foot.

For wider feet

If you have a wide forefoot, or bony prominences like bunions, this system of skipping the lowest eyelets on the shoe may work for you.

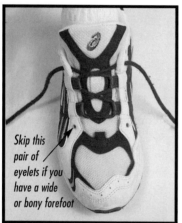

Skip this pair of eyelets if you have a wide or bony forefoot

Simply begin your lacing process one or sometimes two holes up from the bottom. This will allow the upper of the shoe to be a bit more flexible in that area of your forefoot and may help alleviate some pressure. Unfortunately it will also compromise the stability of the shoe in the forefoot region, so if you tend to pronate excessively this may not be the best choice for you. It is always best to try to purchase shoes that are wide enough for your feet without having to change the laces. Thankfully many shoe manufacturers are now offering their most popular styles in various widths. Ask your shoe salesperson for help in finding the shoe with the widest toe box. For women with wide feet, an alternative is to ask for men's shoes as they are built on a somewhat wider last.

For high instep

For the problem of bony prominences on the top of the foot in the area of the instep, or for those with a particularly high instep, sometimes it helps to skip an eyelet or two along the way. Simply lace your shoe as usual, but skip the area of the foot that has been uncomfortable.

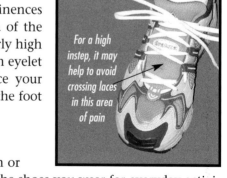

For a high instep, it may help to avoid crossing laces in this area of pain

Everyday footwear

In addition to the shoes you run or walk in, you need to take a look at the shoes you wear for everyday activities. Gravity never takes a day off and the stress imposed by performing normal activities of daily living in a shoe that offers inadequate support may be slowing your healing process. For women who must wear dress shoes to work, the choices are sparse. There are few women's dress shoes that offer the characteristics of good fit, cushioning and motion control. If you're injured, the best choice is to wear your running shoes as much as possible, but for some that isn't an option. Try to select a shoe with the lowest heel and the roomiest toe box. An elevated heel not only places you at greater risk for an ankle sprain or fracture, but it increases the incidence of lower back pain and contributes to a shortening of the calf muscles over time. In addition to this, the elevation of the heel places a greater amount and duration of force through the relatively smaller bones of the forefoot. The fashionably pointed toe boxes contribute to the formation of corns and calluses as well as bunions, neuromas, hammer toes and claw toes. Just buying a low heeled or flat shoe is a good start toward healthier feet and legs. The more the shoe resembles your running shoe (lace up, fairly stiff) the better. In this regard, men have an easier time. Many men's shoes are lace-up, oxford style shoes with relatively stiff soles and uppers. These offer good support. Loafers on the other hand, though low heeled, are usually a poor choice. The fixed amount of room (no laces) usually doesn't allow for orthotic use and the low profile of the upper doesn't offer much support.

> ➊ *Gravity never takes a day off and the stress imposed by performing normal activities of daily living in a shoe that offers inadequate support may be slowing your healing process.*

Orthotics

Sometimes a shoe alone isn't enough to control the amount, timing or speed of pronation. In these cases or cases where there is a significant asymmetry of motion or alignment from one side to the other, or in the case of individuals with a very high arch, an orthotic may be indicated. Over-the-counter arch supports may help a few athletes with mild pronation or a need for a little more cushioning, but often a custom-built device is needed. Controlling the timing and amount of pronation is a delicate balancing act. Too much control is sometimes as troublesome as not enough. To properly address these issues, the practitioner that fabricates the orthotic needs an extensive knowledge of anatomy and biomechanics. The evaluation for orthotics should include an assessment of flexibility and skeletal alignment from the waist all the way down to the toes, as well as a dynamic assessment of your gait pattern both barefoot and in your shoes. With this information in mind, the practitioner can then determine the amount of pronation to control and at what point in the gait cycle to address it. Remember, timing is everything. In order to insure the proper fit of the device, a neutral-position mold is made of your foot using plaster of Paris or a foam material. This mold becomes the template around which the orthotic is fabricated. Orthotics can be made from many materials ranging in characteristics from very soft to very rigid. In most cases, the more motion you're trying to control the more rigid the device will be. After all, it has to withstand the impact of running, which can be 2-5 times body weight. If you can flatten it with your hands, how will it ever support your body weight?

Fabrication of an orthotic is both art and science. The science part comes when all the various measurements of flexibility and skeletal alignment are taken during your evaluation. The art part comes when the practitioner takes all those measurements and combines it with a visual (or computerized) analysis of your gait. The goal is to use the least possible amount of intervention to alleviate your symptoms, rather than trying to take away all your motion. Adjustments to the device are sometimes needed after they are fabricated. Subtle areas of pressure or discomfort will be addressed and the motion controlling characteristics of the device may be adjusted one or more times before the final result is acceptable. Communication with your health care provider is crucial here. The orthotic directly affects motion in the foot and since the foot is attached to the leg, motion will be affected all the way up the kinetic chain. A gradual transition into wearing the orthotic device will usually allow your body to adapt to the new position successfully. However, if things don't feel right, make sure to call the practitioner that fabricated the orthotics and schedule an appointment for an adjustment.

> ❍ *Fabrication of an orthotic is both art and science. The science part comes when all the various measurements of flexibility and skeletal alignment are taken during your evaluation. The art part comes when the practitioner takes all those measurements and combines it with a visual (or computerized) analysis of your gait. The goal is to use the least possible amount of intervention to alleviate your symptoms, rather than trying to take away all your motion.*

Wearing your orthotics full time, in both your athletic and everyday shoes is often the best option. Depending on the demands of your job or daily activities you can be logging some serious mileage during the day, and remember gravity never takes a day off. If you have a fairly sedentary job however, you may be able to get away with wearing the orthotics only in your running shoes. Discuss your options with your health care provider to ascertain your specific needs. Just remember, orthotics are kind of like eyeglasses – they only help you when you're wearing them.

Let's look now at a few of the more common running and walking injuries, then we'll move from the top of the injury prevention pyramid to the bottom and take a look at the role of flexibility and strength in the prevention of these injuries.

REFERENCES CHAPTER ONE

1. Brukner P. *Exercise-related lower leg pain: bone.* Med Sci Sports Exerc. Vol. 32, No. 3, pp. S15-S26, 2000.
2. Kortebein PM, Kaufman KR, Basford JR, Stuart MJ. *Medial tibial stress syndrome.* Med Sci Sports Exerc. Vol. 32, No. 3, pp. S27-S33, 2000.
3. Munro CF, Miller DI, Fuglevand AJ. *Ground reaction forces in running: A reexamination.* J Biomech 20:147-155, 1987.
4. Pietrocarlo TA. *Foot pain in runners.* In Guten GN (ed) Running Injuries. WB Saunders, Philadelphia, 1997, pp. 152-172.
5. Pink MM, Jobe FW. *The foot/shoe interface.* In Guten GN (ed) Running Injuries. WB Saunders, Philadelphia, 1997, pp. 20-29.
6. Root ML, Orien WP, Weed JH. *Normal and Abnormal Function of the Foot.* Clinical Biomechanics Corp., Los Angeles, 1977.

BIBLIOGRAPHY

1. Gray G W. *Lower Extremity Functional Profile.* Wynn Marketing, 1995.
2. Gould, JA. *Orthopedic and Sports Physical Therapy, 2nd Ed.* C.V. Mosby Co. St Louis, 1990.
3. Root ML, Orien WP, Weed JH, Hughes RJ. *Biomechanical Examination of the Foot.* Clinical Biomechanics Publishers, Los Angeles, 1977.

CHAPTER TWO

COMMON RUNNING / WALKING INJURIES

As mentioned in the beginning of this book, injuries can often be traced back to one or more precipitating or causative factors. Although research hasn't *conclusively* confirmed that these factors are always involved, the evidence strongly points to the relationship of these more common factors to the onset of overuse injuries.

1. **Training errors**

2. **Inappropriate footwear**

3. **Inadequate flexibility**

4. **Inadequate strength**

5. **Poor biomechanics**

Rarely are injuries due to just one of these factors, more commonly it is a combination of them. Likewise, injuries are rarely "fixed" by changing only one thing; usually a comprehensive approach is required. By understanding some of the more common injuries, a sensible approach to self-treatment can be initiated early and further injury can sometimes be avoided altogether. Generally, ignoring an injury invites more problems. If treated early with rest, ice and a sensible approach to resumption of training, many injuries can be effectively managed allowing the athlete to return to training fairly quickly. The sooner you treat, the quicker you can return to your activity. **There are often many different diagnoses that can cause similar symptoms so checking with your medical professional for correct diagnosis is crucial.** It is hard to treat the cause for the symptoms if you don't know the diagnosis! Differentiating between tendinosis, peritendonitis, bursitis, stress fractures, arthritic joint changes, and the like will insure that you treat the appropriate problem in the appropriate fashion.

Treatment of symptoms is often directed at alleviation of inflammation, as the inflammatory process has long been believed to be involved in most overuse injuries. Medications, both over-the-counter and prescription have been used to combat inflammation. Some of the more common of these are ibuprofen, naproxyn sodium, aspirin, and various other non-steroidal anti-inflammatory drugs (NSAID's). Injection of corticosteroids has also been used to combat inflammation. Though injection into a tendon is considered controversial by most, some physicians will inject into the area around a tendon in an attempt to alleviate symptoms that are attributed to inflammation. However, a new understanding of the pathology involved in many overuse injuries of tendons sheds a new light on the need for understanding what you're trying to combat. Recent advances in the microscopic evaluation of tissue from chronically injured tendons shows that rather than an inflammatory process being present the actual presentation is more of a degenerative process[20]. In other words, the more common diagnosis of tendinitis, ("itis" being the Greek root word for inflammation) is often incorrect – there are often no inflammatory cells present in the tissue. The cells that are present and visible are *not* inflammatory cells but instead are myofibroblasts (cells which are precursors to muscle and connective tissue). In fact a recent review of research showed that the overwhelming majority of the studies that microscopically evaluated tendons from humans suffering from various overuse injuries showed a degenerative lesion *without* any inflammatory component[2]. The more correct diagnosis then appears to be tendinosis (a degeneration of the collagen fibers that make up the tendon). This is more than semantics here. Understanding the pathology involved may well change the treatment[27]. The degeneration of the collagen matrix of the tendon leads to a weakening of the tissue and an increased risk for subsequent further damage or even rupture. Knowing this makes rest an even more important initial intervention. Further, if the pathology is indeed a degenerative one rather than an inflammatory one – use of corticosteroid injection (which *inhibits* collagen repair) seems clearly to be a poor choice[20]. In fact it is not known if the commonly prescribed NSAID's help or hinder the tendon repair process through mechanisms or pathways other than those associated with inflammation. Clearly this area will continue to be a hot bed of research both in the exercise science and pharmaceutical arenas.

> The degeneration of the collagen matrix of the tendon leads to a weakening of the tissue and an increased risk for subsequent further damage or even rupture. Knowing this makes rest an even more important initial intervention.

Treatment of tendinosis and various other tendinopathies and overuse injuries should focus not only on alleviation of symptoms but primarily on discovering the underlying causative and precipitating factors. Treatment with ice appears to be fairly well accepted as appropriate, and the use of electrotherapy (e.g. high voltage galvanic stimulation) has been shown to stimulate collagen synthesis in the laboratory setting so it may hold some promise as a useful modality[15] (though clinical research is inconclusive on this). Rest and moderating the load on the affected tissue will be beneficial. So in addition to reducing activity level, the use of various supports, braces, orthoses, and lifts is often indicated to mediate the load on the involved tissue. Again, it is important to know the underlying causative factors in order to understand what to support or brace. Appropriate flexibility and strength training exercises are almost always indicated. Recent research confirms earlier studies that show that eccentric strength training exercises (like those described later in Chapter 4) stimulate collagen production and promote proper alignment and cross linking of collagen fibers – hence enhancing the tendon strength[1]. **Finally it must be emphasized that the healing process takes time and that early return to activity while the tissue remains weakened from a degenerative process may not only impair the body's ability to repair damaged tissue, but may indeed lead to further damage. Patience is truly a virtue in this regard.**

In the following pages a few of the more common injuries are reviewed. This is by no means an exhaustive review of the myriad of injuries that may occur but only an overview of the more common ones. *It is imperative that athletes consult with their physician or other health care provider for conclusive diagnosis and formulation of a rehabilitation plan.* The information here is provided only to help the athlete understand some of the underlying factors involved in some of the more common injuries and is not intended to substitute for sound medical advice or treatment.

HEEL PAIN

There can be many causes for heel pain; probably the most common diagnosis is Plantar Fasciitis. Literally speaking, this is an inflammation ("itis") of the fascia on the plantar (bottom) surface of the foot. This fascia (also called the plantar aponeurosis) attaches to the heel bone at one end and the junction of the toes to the metatarsals (ball of the foot) at the other end. When your foot pronates upon contact with the ground, the bones that form your arch "unlock" so that your foot can absorb shock and adapt to uneven terrain (see chapter one for further details on the biomechanics of gait). As your arch flattens, the plantar fascia is stretched. If your calf muscle is a little tight, it places additional stress on the plantar fascia as your heel comes up off the ground.

The most common symptom is pain in the bottom of the heel when first arising in the morning or after being seated for a period of time. Though somewhat less common, pain may also occur in other areas of the heel, and sometimes a "tearing" sensation is felt in the arch of the foot. The pain usually dissipates relatively quickly with activity and in some cases may return later in the day after prolonged standing. Many people describe the first symptoms as feeling like a "stone bruise" on the bottom of the foot. Left untreated, these symptoms often progress to the point where acute pain is present with nearly all activity. X-rays may or may not reveal a spur on the heel bone, and the spur if present may not be the source of the pain. Some studies have shown that 15% of feet with no symptoms display heel spurring on x-ray.[9]

Possible factors involved:

- Tight calf muscles (other leg muscles may also be involved)
- Inadequate support from the running shoe
- Training errors (too many hills, too much speed too soon, adding mileage too quickly)
- Biomechanical factors (excessive or prolonged pronation, or high arched and rigid "cavus" feet)

Treatment strategies:

- Stretch calf muscles (3-5 times per day is helpful)
- Examine shoes for wear and appropriate motion control and cushioning characteristics & replace frequently
- Ice (10 minutes 2-3 times/day if possible)
- Adjust training schedule (decrease speedwork & hills, reduce total mileage per week)
- Physical therapy – may include deep tissue massage to the calf, cross friction massage to the foot or lower leg, various exercises to stretch and strengthen, and modalities to improve blood flow through the area.
- Resting night splints
- Orthotics to control excessive or poorly timed pronation, or to support high arch

A few other conditions that may cause similar pain – see your physician for a proper diagnosis.

- Fat pad atrophy – a deterioration of the fat pad that lies under the heel bone.
- Plantar fascia rupture – a partial (or complete) tear of the plantar fascia.

- Tarsal tunnel syndrome – similar to the more well known "carpal tunnel syndrome"; this is an irritation of the nerves as they course through the tarsal tunnel.
- Nerve entrapment
- Stress fracture – though less common than stress fractures of the tibia, this is also a possibility.
- Tumor

ACHILLES TENDINOPATHY

This is an overuse injury of the Achilles tendon. Frequently referred to as Achilles Tendinitis, it has been shown that often the condition is more of a degenerative tendinosis than it is an inflammatory tendinitis[20]. This large tendon attaches your calf muscle group (including the Gastrocnemius and Soleus) to your heel bone, and is a common site of injury in athletes. One of the primary factors leading to Achilles tendon injury is the force that the tendon is subjected to when excessive pronation takes place[6.] This rotational force not only places a tensile demand on the tendon but also has been theorized to further restrict blood flow in a crucial area of the tendon that already has limited blood flow. The first symptoms can be soreness in the tendon first thing in the morning or a vague, dull, aching in the tendon after running[17.] There is also frequently stiffness and aching in the tendon upon first arising in the morning. If ignored, the symptoms usually worsen to the point where pain is present on the initiation of running and increases with sprinting, though symptoms may get better in the course of the run. Untreated, the symptoms eventually become present at all times and the individual is unable to run due to acute pain, and may be unable to walk without pain. Although one primary factor related to most Achilles tendinopathies is lack of flexibility in the calf muscle group, stretching these muscles when in an acute flare up will only make things worse. **This is one time when stretching must be delayed until the acute soreness has subsided.** If the symptoms are caught early, a short rest of about 2 weeks will often settle things down. If stretching can be accomplished without pain occurring in the tendon during the course of the stretch, then stretching is appropriate. If the stretch causes discomfort in the tendon, then stretching must be delayed. Pain that has been

> ➧ *Although one primary factor related to most Achilles tendinopathies is lack of flexibility in the calf muscle group, stretching these muscles when in an acute flare up will only make things worse. This is one time when stretching must be delayed until the acute soreness has subsided.*

present for more than 3 to 6 weeks usually requires 6 weeks or more of rest to resolve. A thickening and scarring of the Achilles tendon, making it weaker and at greater risk of rupture in the future, often accompanies symptoms that persist for 8 or more weeks[22].

Possible factors involved:

- Tight calf muscles (as well as hip flexors and other leg muscles)
- Excessive shoe wear, allowing for excessive pronation, or shoes with an inappropriate amount of motion control. Note that shoes that are too rigid as well as shoes that are too soft have been indicated in the onset of this condition. It pays to get the shoe that is correct for your biomechanics!
- Too much speed work too soon
- Too much hill work too soon
- Increasing mileage too quickly
- Biomechanical faults including excessive or poorly timed pronation, and rigid "cavus" (high arched) feet

Treatment strategies:

- Small heel lift for temporary relief until symptoms subside, then stretch (heel lifts should be used on both sides to avoid causing other problems such as lower back pain.)
- REST
- Reduce speed work and hills, and reduce total mileage per week
- ICE after training
- Physical Therapy – which may include deep tissue massage to the calf muscle group, cross friction massage, modalities to improve circulation, and instruction in various stretching and strength training exercises.
- Resting night splints
- Massage therapy

A few other conditions that may cause similar pain – see your physician for a proper diagnosis.

- Retrocalcaneal bursitis – an inflammation of the bursa that lies underneath the Achilles tendon.
- Peritendinitis – an inflammation of the sheath that surrounds the Achilles tendon.

- Tendinosis – a degenerative process.
- Partial or complete rupture – this is a significant problem requiring immediate attention. Surgical repair of the tendon is often necessary.

KNEE PAIN

One common term used to describe knee pain in runners is "Runner's Knee". Really a catchall term, this refers to pain in and around the kneecap or "patella". This odd shaped bone is an integral part of the quadriceps muscle on the front of the thigh. The patella glides in a groove on the femur (thigh bone) and acts as a fulcrum to improve the angle of pull of the quadriceps muscle, which attaches to the lower leg bone (tibia) through a thick tendon, called the patellar tendon. The quadriceps muscle is very active in running and walking, especially when going downhill. The early symptoms are often a dull aching in and around the patella, after exercise. There may be stiffness in the knee as well, partly due to a swelling of the irritated tissues. Depending on the biomechanics of the individual athlete, the pain may be localized to one area or another of the knee. If the pain is more general or centrally located in the patellar tendon it is often diagnosed as **Patellar Tendinitis or Tendinosis, or Patello-femoral Pain Syndrome.** If the biomechanics of the athlete are such that the patella does not sit properly in its femoral groove, the underside of the patella may wear down over time and become rough and deteriorated. This condition is known as **Chondromalacia Patella**[13]. In the past it was theorized that one of the main causes of this condition (and many others involving the patella) was an imbalance of strength between the individual muscles that make up the quadriceps muscle group, in particular the Vastus Medialis Oblique (VMO) and it's anatomical opposite the Vastus Lateralis. Detailed studies using sensitive equipment to measure the electrical activity of the various muscles that make up the quadriceps group have since shown that although this theory is appealing, it is in fact <u>not</u> the case. [29, 24, 30, 21.]

Possible factors involved:

- Limited flexibility (quadriceps, hamstrings, calves)
- Biomechanical faults (usually excessive or prolonged pronation)
- Worn or improper shoes
- Training errors – too much hill work too soon, too much speed work, increasing mileage too quickly
- Muscle weakness (most probably in the hips and thighs)

Treatment strategies:

- Stretch tight muscles
- Examine shoes for wear, appropriate motion control characteristics and replace frequently
- ICE
- Rest, and reduce hill work and speed work and total mileage per week
- Physical Therapy – which may include various stretching and strength training exercises as well as modalities to improve circulation through injured tissues.
- Orthotics to control excessive or poorly timed pronation
- Strength training (generally the hip muscles as well as the thigh muscles). Note that some authors promote specific strength training of the Vastus Medialis Oblique (VMO) fibers of the quadriceps group but electromyographic studies (EMG) have not shown that selective strengthening of these fibers separate from the rest of the quadriceps group is possible.
- Massage therapy – deep tissue massage to the muscles that are tight may enhance your ability to regain your flexibility

A few other conditions that may cause similar pain[13] - see your physician for proper diagnosis.

- Bursitis – an irritation of the bursa that lies beneath the patella.
- Peritendonitis – an inflammation of the sheath that surrounds the Patellar tendon.
- Ligament strain or sprain – usually there is a traumatic event to cause this, but not always.
- Meniscal tears or degeneration – the menisci are the cartilages within the knee joint that act to both increase the stability of the joint and to cushion the bones of the femur (thigh) and tibia (lower leg) from impact.

MEDIAL TIBIAL STRESS SYNDROME ("SHIN SPLINTS")

More commonly known as "shin splints", this is probably one of the most common complaints of beginning runners and walkers. The term "shin splints" is somewhat of a catchall term for several more specific diagnoses so it won't be used here as it lacks specificity. The source of pain has been theorized to be inflammation of the attachment points of one or more muscles including the Posterior Tibialis, the Soleus, and the

Flexor Digitorum Longus where their tendons attach to the outer covering of the bone known as the periosteum. Initially it was thought that the Posterior Tibialis muscle was the one most likely involved, and the term Posterior Tibial Shin Splints was used, but more recent research points toward the Soleus or Flexor Digitorum Longus muscles as being the likely culprits[7]. Symptoms usually consist of an aching that occurs along and just behind the front surface of the shinbone (hence the name *medial tibial* stress syndrome). The pain is fairly diffuse in nature, covering a region that may be several centimeters in length, in contrast to a stress fracture that presents with more localized point tenderness, or to compartment syndrome which presents with aching that resolves with rest. Initially the pain occurs when you first run or walk, and may subside later in the exercise bout only to return later. At this early stage, the symptoms resolve relatively quickly with rest. When training is resumed, if the underlying factors contributing to the problem have not been addressed, the symptoms return and over time become more severe and chronic in nature.

➲ *When training is resumed, if the underlying factors contributing to the problem have not been addressed, the symptoms return and over time become more severe and chronic in nature.*

As the condition worsens, the symptoms are present with nearly all activities and may also present as a tenderness and stiffness when first arising[23]. There may be localized tenderness to the touch and there may also be some swelling. If there is acute and localized tenderness, a physician may use a bone scan to rule out a stress fracture. The factors most associated with medial tibial stress syndrome are training errors[14] (primarily excessive mileage, hills or intensity) and faulty biomechanics (primarily excessive or poorly timed pronation[32]). Lack of adequate flexibility of the calf muscles also plays a significant role due to its tendency to accentuate pronation when tight.

Possible factors involved:

- ✱ Training errors (too much emphasis on hill work or speed work too soon, or increasing mileage too quickly)
- ✱ Biomechanical faults (excessive or prolonged pronation)
- ✱ Tight calf muscles
- ✱ Excessive shoe wear, or use of shoes that do not offer the appropriate motion control characteristics

Treatment strategies:

- ✱ Stretch tight calf muscles (several times a day is good)

- Decrease mileage and hill work / speedwork
- Assess shoe for appropriate motion control characteristics, wear and replace frequently
- ICE
- Physical Therapy – which may include deep tissue massage to the calf muscle group, stretching and strength training exercises, and various modalities to improve circulation to healing tissues.

A few other conditions that may cause similar pain[10] – see your physician for proper diagnosis.

- Stress fracture – this can be diagnosed through the use of a bone scan. Standard X-rays often miss stress fractures until healing has taken place.
- Chronic exertional compartment syndrome – see the next section for details
- Referred pain from lumbar spine
- Nerve or artery entrapment
- Tumors

CHRONIC EXERTIONAL COMPARTMENT SYNDROME

The muscles of the lower leg are separated by fascia into 5 "compartments". With exercise, the muscles increase in size due to an increase in blood flow and with repeated bouts of exercise over time they will hypertrophy (grow larger). The common theory regarding this diagnosis is that as the muscle increases in size, it takes up more space in its "compartment" and thus the pressure within the compartment is increased and the blood flow to the muscle is decreased. Although clearly an increase in compartment pressure can be documented, recent research has shown that the blood flow is <u>not</u> consistently significantly restricted[3,4]. Other theories as to why there is pain associated with the high compartment pressures include a stimulation of the sensory receptors on the fascia or periosteum (covering of the bone), or a biochemical change due to the marginally decreased blood flow[4]. Regardless of the true cause of the pain, one fact remains – surgical release of the fascia in the affected compartments is almost always successful in alleviating the symptoms. The classic symptoms of this condition are a cramping, burning or aching sensation that comes on consistently at a certain time into an exercise bout. The symptoms persist or even increase as exercise is continued, but resolve shortly after ceasing activity. There is classically no discomfort at rest, and generally no tenderness to touch[8]. Diagnosis is made by symptom presentation, and is confirmed by checking the pressures within the various compartments at rest and immediately following an activity that brings on the symptoms. Normally pressures will return to a resting level within 3-5 minutes after stopping exercise, therefore a delay of longer than 6 minutes in returning to resting pressure levels is considered a positive test[31]. Factors that could be involved in the onset of this syndrome include excessive and/ or prolonged pronation, complicated by limited flexibility of the calf muscle, though no research has yet shown these factors to be consistently present in all cases. It stands to reason that if the foot/leg is going through excessive pronation, the muscles that help to decelerate this motion will be under an increased stress and will likely undergo compensatory adaptation (get larger, hypertrophy) to

> ➊ *The classic symptoms of this condition are a cramping, burning or aching sensation that comes on consistently at a certain time into an exercise bout. The symptoms persist or even increase as exercise is continued, but resolve shortly after ceasing activity. There is classically no discomfort at rest, and generally no tenderness to touch[8].*

accommodate. If this is the case, the subsequent increase in muscle size may play a role in the onset of the symptoms. Though little research has been done on conservative treatment for this condition, some researchers have shown that deep tissue massage and orthotic intervention may be beneficial in some cases if caught early enough[19]. Clearly the most research has been done on surgical interventions and the reality is that for many athletes this is the only cure. Depending on the compartment(s) released a return to full activity can be anticipated within 8 - 16 weeks post-operatively.

Possible factors involved:

- ✖ Biomechanical faults – excessive or prolonged pronation, high arched rigid ("cavus") feet or flat feet
- ✖ Training errors – too much too soon, too many hills, too much speedwork
- ✖ Genetic predisposition
- ✖ Limited flexibility in muscles of lower leg

Treatment strategies:

- ✖ REST
- ✖ Stretch tight muscles

- Correct biomechanical faults through footwear or orthotic intervention
- Deep tissue massage
- Surgery to release involved fascial compartments

A few other conditions that may cause lower leg pain[8] - see your physician for proper diagnosis.

- Entrapment of various arteries or nerves
- Stress fracture – see description below.
- Periostitis – irritation of the periosteum (covering of the bone).
- Tenosynovitis – inflammation of a tendon sheath
- Infection
- Tumor
- Traction periostitis – irritation of the perisoteum at the attachment point of various muscle groups.

STRESS FRACTURES

Stress fractures are partial or complete cracks in the outer layers of the bone that occur as a result of repetitive stress. It has been reported that 70% of all stress fractures occur in runners[12]. Generally they occur in the lower limbs, but can occur anywhere there is a chronic pattern of excessive stress. In runners (and to a lesser extent walkers), the common sites for stress fractures include tibia (shinbone), metatarsals (long bones of the foot) and calcaneus (heel bone), with the most common site being the tibia[12,25]. In addition, the femur (thighbone), the navicular bone (in your foot), the fibula (lower lateral leg bone), and occasionally the pelvis and sacrum may also be affected. The symptoms of a stress fracture include pain that is worst when exercising but may also be present at rest. The pain is generally quite localized to a specific bony area and is most noticeable when the area is pressed or tapped. What specifically causes stress fractures is the subject of some debate. One theory suggests that muscles fatigued by repetitive exercise lose some of their shock absorbing ability, placing a both a greater magnitude and rate of strain on the bone and eventually leading to a fracture[33]. Another theory implies that the repetitive stress does not allow bone adequate time to respond to the strain. Bone responds to strain by remodeling

> **◑** The symptoms of a stress fracture include pain that is worst when exercising but may also be present at rest. The pain is generally quite localized to a specific bony area and is most noticeable when the area is pressed or tapped.

and this process begins with a resorption (breakdown) of bone and subsequent rebuilding phase. If an adequate amount of time is not allowed for this rebuilding process, then subsequent strain on the now weakened bone will lead to micro-fractures, and over time to a breakdown and fracture[28]. Though this theory has not been proven conclusively it is reasonable in light of the incidence of stress fractures occurring within 3-7 weeks after initiation of vigorous training or a sudden increase in training. The time-table for bone remodeling is as follows: the resorption phase lasts about 3 weeks and the formation or rebuilding phase follows over the next 3 months[12]. Whatever the physiological mechanism may be, the physical causes are usually related to training errors and biomechanical factors. Other factors to be considered are a low bone mineral density caused by insufficient dietary calcium and hormonal insufficiencies (low blood estrogen in women[5,26]). Routine X-rays are often inconclusive and true diagnosis must often be made through the use of a bone scan. Treatment for stress fractures consists of a period of active rest that may last 4-7 weeks and in some cases up to 3 months or more. During this time the athlete may be allowed some weight bearing on the affected leg, but generally will be restricted from any aggressive weight bearing activity. In addition, the athlete may be encouraged by the physician to take supplemental calcium (up to 1500 mg. per day[11]). Once the stress fracture has healed, the return to activity must be slow enough to allow the bone adequate time to adapt successfully to the stresses imposed.

Possible factors involved:

- **Training errors** – abrupt changes in training, mileage, intensity, duration, or equipment.
- **Biomechanical faults** – excessive or poorly timed pronation, rigid ("cavus") high arched feet, or flexible ("planus") flat feet.
- Low bone mineral density (menstrual irregularities)
- Genetics – small cross sectional area of tibia bone
- Lack of adequate muscular strength

Treatment strategies:

- REST
- **Biomechanical evaluation and gait / shoe analysis with orthotic intervention as needed**
- Address training errors
- Supplemental calcium as directed by physician and avoidance of

diet soft drinks and a high protein diet which may inhibit the body's ability to absorb calcium

- Strength training for weak muscles, flexibility exercises for tight muscles
- Cross training during period of healing to maintain cardiovascular fitness levels

A few other conditions that may cause similar pain – see your physician for proper diagnosis.

- Osteoid osteoma – a particular type of bony tumor.
- Periostitis – an irritation of the sheath that surrounds the bone.

ILIOTIBIAL BAND FRICTION SYNDROME

Iliotibial Band Syndrome (ITBS) is an irritation of the Iliotibial Band (ITB), most commonly at the point where it courses over the lateral femoral condyle (the side of the knee) or at its insertion below the knee[16]. The Iliotibial Band is a long, thick band of fascia that runs from the outer hip area to the outside of the knee and attaches to the lower leg bone (the lateral tibia) just below the knee joint. It attaches to large muscles of the lateral (outside) hip, including the Gluteus Medius and Tensor Fascia. It crosses both the hip joint and the knee joint and hence it is important in the actions of both. Its function in gait is dynamic and changes with the position of the knee joint. Initially it acts to decelerate the inward rotation of the leg and flexion (bending) of the knee that occurs in conjunction with pronation of the foot. As the knee flexes beyond a certain point, the angle of pull changes and the Iliotibial band now functions to assist the Hamstrings in flexion of the knee in the swing phase of gait. The symptoms of ITBS include discomfort in the lower outside thigh or knee area that initially presents only during activity. The tenderness is usually well localized and swelling is usually not present or is minimal. If left untreated the symptoms may gradually worsen to the point where they are present with almost all activity. One popular misconception is that only "supinators" get this problem. Nothing could be farther from the truth. More commonly the excessive internal rotation of the leg that accompanies pronation is the cause for the problem as the ITB is a decelerator of this internal rotation. Though in rare cases it is brought on by

> ● *The symptoms of ITBS include discomfort in the lower outside thigh or knee area that initially presents only during activity. The tenderness is usually well localized and swelling is usually not present or is minimal.*

33

chronically running on the same slant of the road, (the leg that is on the down-slope is most affected) it is much more commonly seen in athletes with either poor biomechanics or poor flexibility and strength (or both).

Possible Factors Involved:

- **Poor Biomechanics** – usually excessive or poorly timed pronation
- Inadequate flexibility – Especially calf muscles, buttock muscles, lateral hip muscles and outer thigh muscles. Hamstrings and quadriceps may also be involved.
- Training errors – always running the same slope of the road, excessive speed work, too much mileage, sudden change in training, excessive hill work.
- Excessive shoe wear, or inappropriate shoe choices

Treatment Strategies:

- **Address Biomechanical issues through change in footwear or orthotics as needed**
- Stretch tight calf muscles, hamstrings and hips
- Decrease mileage, speedwork, and hill training
- Replace worn shoes
- ICE
- Physical Therapy – which may include deep tissue massage to tight areas in the gluteals and hamstrings as well as stretching and strength training exercises and various modalities to improve blood flow to healing tissues.
- Deep tissue massage
- Strengthen weak muscles – especially the hips

A few other conditions that may cause similar symptoms – see your physician for proper diagnosis.

- Lateral collateral ligament strain – this is the ligament that supports the lateral side of the knee joint. There is usually a precipitating traumatic event, but not always.
- Osteoarthritic conditions – degeneration of the joint over a period of time.
- Meniscal lesions – disruption of the menisci (cartilages) within the knee joint. This can be traumatic, or can occur over a period of time (wear and tear).

✕ Insertional tendinitis of the lateral hamstring muscle – irritation of the hamstring tendon where it attaches to the lower leg bone.

FOREFOOT PAIN

Several different diagnoses may be responsible for pain in the forefoot region. This part of your foot withstands the greatest amount of ground reaction force every step – and is not surprisingly a fairly common area of pain for runners and walkers. The metatarsals are the bones in your foot that correspond to the bones in the palm of your hand. They run from about the middle of the arch to the ball of your foot where they attach to the toes.

Metatarsalgia is the term used to describe pain in the ball of the foot. Some of the common causes of this pain include Morton's Neuroma (described later), stress fractures, synovitis (an irritation of the synovium or lubricating tissue for a joint), and arthritis. In addition to tight calf muscles, one of the most common factors involved in metatarsal pain is a poorly fitted shoe[18]. If the toe box of the shoe is either too short or too narrow it compresses the metatarsals and not only interferes with their natural biomechanics but may also place pressure on the interdigital nerves, causing a condition known as **Morton's Neuroma.** The nerve most commonly affected is the third interdigital nerve, between the third and fourth metatarsal[18].

The symptoms of **Morton's Neuroma** are usually a burning, cramping and tingling sensation in the toes. There is generally tenderness in the space between the metatarsals and pinching this area between the thumb and forefinger while squeezing the forefoot with the other hand will usually produce significant discomfort. Symptoms can sometimes be relieved by removing the shoes, only to return again the next time that the shoes are worn or during the next exercise bout. Some people describe the early sensation as feeling as if their socks have "wadded up" under the ball of the foot. Left untreated, symptoms can become more frequent and intense, eventually causing discomfort with most activities.

> ◗ The symptoms of Morton's Neuroma are usually a burning, cramping and tingling sensation in the toes. There is generally tenderness in the space between the metatarsals

The symptoms of a **metatarsal stress fracture** on the other hand are usually a more localized point tenderness of the specific metatarsal. The symptoms may start as an aching sensation under the ball of the foot (where the toes join the foot). In the early stages, rest may alleviate the symptoms but as the condition worsens the pain becomes present even while walking or at rest[18]. Though x-rays will often be negative, a bone scan will successfully diagnose a stress fracture as early as 48-72 hours after the onset of symptoms. Several weeks of rest will be required to allow the bone to heal, and the underlying factors that contributed to the stress fracture should be addressed to avoid recurrence of the problem. As with other stress fractures, training errors and biomechanical issues are the key factors involved.

Sesamoid pathology may be another cause of forefoot pain. The sesamoid bones are two small bones situated under the first metatarsal, contained within the tendon of the flexor hallucis brevis muscle. The athlete will complain of pain and/or swelling under the joint where the great toe joins the foot. Bending the great toe back generally makes this pain worse. Several different diagnoses may be made including sesamoid stress fracture, bursitis, acute fracture, osteochondritis, arthritis, and sesamoiditis. Fractures and stress fractures will require several weeks of rest and may require surgery if healing does not take place. Generally conservative care and addressing the underlying biomechanical factors involved will allow healing, and an eventual return to activity.

Hallux limitus and/or **hallux rigidus** – these two diagnoses refer to a gradual loss of flexibility in the joint of the great toe. Symptoms generally present as distinct aching or pain in the region of the great toe joint. Sometimes use of special supports or shoes with stiffer soles will offer relief, but generally the process is a degenerative one and surgery may eventually be required.

Possible factors involved

- **Poorly fitted shoes, or shoes that do not offer appropriate motion control and cushioning characteristics**
- Inadequate flexibility in calf muscles
- **Biomechanical issues** – excessive or prolonged pronation, rigid high arched ("cavus") foot type, or excessively mobile low arched ("planus") foot type.
- Excessive shoe wear
- Training errors – excessive or sudden changes in hill work, speed-work, or mileage

Treatment Strategies:

- Insure proper shoe fit (at least one thumb's width between the end of the longest toe and the end of the toe box of the shoe)

- Stretch tight calf muscles
- Replace worn shoes
- Address biomechanical factors through changes in footwear or use of orthotics (or both)
- Rest
- Physical Therapy
- Correct training errors

REFERENCES CHAPTER TWO

1. Alfredson H, Pietilla T, Jonsson T, et al. *Heavy-load eccentric calf muscle training for the treatment of chronic Achilles tendinosis.* Am. J. Sports Med. Vol. 26, No. 3, pp. 360-366, 1998.

2. Almekinders LC, Temple JD. *Etiology, diagnosis, and treatment of tendonitis: an analysis of the literature.* Med. Sci. Sports Exerc. Vol.30, No.8, pp. 1183-1190, 1998.

3. Amedola A, Rorabeck CH, Vellett D, Vezina W, Rutt B, Lott L. *The use of MRI in exertional compartment syndromes.* Am. J. Sports Med. 18:29-34, 1990.

4. Balduini FC, Shenton DW, O'Connor KH, Heppenstall RB. *Chronic exertional compartment syndrome: correlation of compartment pressure and muscle ischemia utilizing P-NMR spectroscopy.* Clin. Sports Med. 12:151-165, 1993.

5. Barrow GW, Saha S. *Menstrual irregularity and stress fractures in collegiate female distance runners.* Am. J. Sports Med. 16:209-216, 1988.

6. Baumhauer JF, Shereff MJ, Gould JS. *Ankle Pain in Runners.* In Guten GN (ed) Running Injuries, WB Saunders, Philadelphia, 1997, pp. 134-151.

7. Beck BR, Osternig LR. *Medial Tibial Stress Syndrome: the location of muscles in the leg in relation to symptoms.* J. Bone Joint Surg. 76A:1057-1061, 1994.

8. Blackman PG. *A review of chronic exertional compartment syndrome in the lower leg.* Med. Sci. Sports Exerc. Vol. 32, No. 3, pp. S4-S10, 2000.

9. Bordelon, R. Luke MD. *Surgical & Conservative Foot Care.* 1988, Slack Inc., p.107.

10. Brukner P. *Exercise-related lower leg pain: an overview.* Med. Sci. Sports Exerc. Vol. 32, No. 3, pp. S1-S3, 2000.

11. Brukner P. *Exercise-related lower leg pain: bone.* Med. Sci. Sports Exerc. Vol. 32, No. 3, pp. S15-S26, 2000.

12. Burr DB. *Bone, Exercise and Stress Fractures.* Exercise and Sports Sciences Reviews, Vol. 25, pp. 171-194. 1997.

13. Foos GR, Fox JM. *Arthroscopy of the Knee in Runners.* In Guten GN (ed) Running Injuries, WB Saunders, Philadelphia, 1997, pp. 93-111.

14. Fredericson M, Bergman AG, Hoffman KL, Dillingham MS. *Tibial stress reaction in runners.* Am. J. Sports Med. 23:472-481, 1995.

15. Gum SL, Reddy GK, Stehno-Bittel L, et al. *Combined ultrasound, electrical stimulation and laser promote collagen synthesis with moderate changes in tendon biomechanics.* Am. J. Phys. Med. Rehabil. Vol.76, No.4, pp. 288-296, 1997.

16. Guten GN. *Overview of Leg Injuries in Running.* In Guten GN (ed) Running Injuries, WB Saunders, Philadelphia, 1997, pp. 61-92.

17. Hawley JA. *Handbook of sports medicine and science: Running.* Blackwell Sciences, Oxford England, 2000, pp. 72-89.

18. Hockenberry, RT. *Forefoot problems in athletes.* Med. Sci Sports Exerc. Vol 31. No. 7, pp. S448-S458, 1999.

19. Hutchison MR, Ireland ML. *Common compartment syndromes in athletes: treatment and rehabilitation.* Sports Med. 17:200-208, 1994.

20. Kahn KM, Cook JL, Taunton JE, Bonar F. *Overuse Tendinosis, Not Tendonitis Part 1: A New Paradigm for a Difficult Clinical Problem.* Phys. and Sportsmed. Vol.28 No.5, pp. 38-47, 2000.

21. Karst GM, Willett GM. *Onset timing of electromyographic activity in the vastus medialis oblique and vastus lateralis muscles in subjects with and without patellofemoral pain syndrome.* Phys. Ther. Vol.75, No. 9, pp. 813-823, 1995.

22. Keene, James S. in *Orthopedic and Sports Physical Therapy 2nd Edition.* Edited by Gould, James A. 1990, C.V. Mosby Co., p 153.

23. Kortebein PM, Kaufman KR, Basford JR, Stuart MJ. *Medial tibial stress syndrome.* Med. Sci. Sports Exerc. Vol. 32, No. 3, pp. S27-S33, 2000.

24. Laprade J, Culham E, Brouwer B. *Comparison of five isometric exercises in the recruitment of the vastus medialis oblique in persons with and without patellofemoral pain syndrome.* J. Orthop. Sports Phys. Ther. Vol. 27, No.3, pp. 197-204, 1998.

25. Leach RE, Zecher SB. Stress Fractures. In Guten GN (ed) Running Injuries, WB Saunders, Philadelphia, 1997, pp. 30-42.

26. Lloyd TS, Triantafyllou SJ, Baker ER, et al. *Women athletes with menstrual irregularity have increased musculoskeletal injuries.* Med. Sci. Sports Exerc. 18:374-379, 1986.

27. Main JD, Wolin P. *Overuse tendon injuries test practitioner mettle.* Biomechanics, June 1999, pp. 47-60.

28. Martin RB. *Mathematical model for repair of fatigue damage and stress fracture in osteonal bone.* J Orthop. Res. 13:309-316, 1995.

29. Mirzabeigi E, Jordan C, Gronley JK, Rockowitz NL, Perry J. *Isolation of the vastus medialis oblique muscle during exercise.* Am. J. Sports Med. Vol. 27, No.1, pp. 50-53, 1999.

30. Powers CM, Landel R, Perry J. *Timing and intensity of vastus muscle activity during functional activities in subjects with and without patellofemoral pain.* Phys. Ther., Vol. 76, No. 9., pp. 956-967, 1996.

31. Rorabeck CH, Bourne RB, Fowler PJ, Finlay JB, Nott L. *The role of tissue pressure measurement in diagnosing chronic anterior compartment syndrome.* Am. J. Sports Med. 16:143-146, 1988.

32. Sommer HM, Vallentyne SW. *Effect of foot posture on the incidence of medial tibial stress syndrome.* Med. Sci. Sports Exerc. 27:800-804, 1995

33. Yoshikawa T, Mori S, Santieseban AJ, et al. *The effects of muscle fatigue on bone strain.* J Exp. Biol. 188:217-233, 1994.

CHAPTER THREE

FLEXIBILITY

Now we move to the bottom of the injury prevention pyramid and look at the role of flexibility in the prevention and rehabilitation of injuries.

Why stretch?

What is the big deal about stretching anyway? You're probably asking yourself "Why should I start now? I've been training for years and never stretched." To put it into perspective, let's look at what your muscles are trying to accomplish when you run and more specifically when you train for an event like a marathon. With each step you take your muscles must contract to absorb the impact forces of your body crashing into the ground and then propel you safely on your way. Let's do the math…if the average running stride length is 3.5 feet that amounts to 1508 steps per mile. Now multiply your body weight times 2.5 – that's roughly the amount of impact force being absorbed at *each* foot strike. So, for a 150-pound individual, that totals 565,500 pounds of impact force *per mile*. Now multiply that by a conservative beginners marathon training schedule of 40 miles per week, you come up with 22,620,000 pounds of impact force per week. Did someone say cumulative trauma? Your muscles must be both flexible and strong to adequately absorb and transform this force into forward momentum. Still not convinced? How about these statistics – Davis reports in "Prevention and Treatment of Running Injuries" that some 92% of injured runners seen in Physical Therapy clinics were found to have inadequate flexibility in one or more muscle groups[2].

> ➊ *Let's do the math…if the average running stride length is 3.5 feet that amounts to 1508 steps per mile. Now multiply your body weight times 2.5 – that's roughly the amount of impact force being absorbed at **each** foot strike. So, for a 150-pound individual, that totals 565,500 pounds of impact force **per mile**. Now multiply that by a conservative beginners marathon-training schedule of 40 miles per week, you come up with 22,620,000 pounds of impact force per week. Did someone say cumulative trauma?*

Plain and simple – if you want to avoid injury one of the best investments you can make is time spent stretching and strengthening your muscles. As with all things in life, there's a right and a wrong way to go about things. You need to stretch the right muscle in the correct fashion to reap the benefit. Here's the low down on how to avoid the pitfalls of incorrect stretching.

When to stretch

Let's set the record straight - if it were <u>dangerous</u> to stretch "cold" every cat and dog in the world would be chronically injured. Now, with that said, it is always more *effective* to stretch a warm muscle and you *DO run a greater risk of injury* when performing *sustained* stretches on cold muscles. With that in mind, **the most effective stretching will be done when your muscles are warm,** like they are after a warm up walk or after a warm shower or soak in the hot tub. Some researchers put the ideal tissue temperature for stretching at about 39^0 C (or about 102^0 F)[4]. Warmth reduces the viscosity of your body fluids, and increases the elasticity of the muscles and connective tissue[3]. The end of your run or walk is also a great time to stretch; your muscles are thoroughly warmed up then. Most people find that if they're trying to overcome an injury it helps to take a stretch break part way through their workout. This is especially true as you begin to return to running or walking after an injury. To do this, warm up for a few moments at a slower than usual pace, then stop and stretch the key muscles <u>very gently.</u> Then resume your workout, starting back at your warm-up pace.

When not to stretch

Sometimes stretching is NOT the thing to do. Generally this is the case immediately following a severe muscle strain or sprain where substantial bruising is apparent within 24 hours of injury. In this case, gentle active motion within a *painfree range* is OK, but trying to "stretch it out" may well make the injury worse. Anytime you are performing a stretch and are feeling a pain or pulling sensation in the "wrong" place (i.e. not where you're supposed to be feeling it) you should re-evaluate your position and decide if it is too soon to stretch. Achilles tendinopathy is a great example of this. Often in a case of Achilles tendinopathy, it is difficult to stretch the calf muscles without feeling the stretch in the Achilles tendon itself. If this is the case, try reducing the intensity of the stretch, and if this reduction in intensity doesn't alleviate the pull in the tendon, then it is too soon to stretch. Stretching immediately after a

> ➲ *Sometimes stretching is NOT the thing to do. Generally this is the case immediately following a severe muscle strain or sprain where substantial bruising is apparent within 24 hours of injury.*

very long run (more than 15 miles) may not be the best time. Give yourself several minutes to walk to bring your heart rate down to normal and rehydrate yourself. Walking for at least a half mile after a 10-15 mile run is a great idea. It should be a gentle stroll, and you should be sipping water or an electrolyte replacement drink throughout this cool down. Then proceed with a few very gentle stretches; paying close attention to avoid over stretching. You should do the bulk of your stretching later in the day, after you've rested and had a shower and something to eat. Then take a few moments to warm up by walking around and proceed as usual with your stretches.

How to stretch

There are three basic methods for stretching: static, ballistic, and PNF (proprioceptive neuromuscular facilitation).[5] Ballistic stretching, where you move a body part rhythmically and rapidly into a stretched position, has a high risk for injury and is less than optimal for the type of flexibility you'll need. Those who participate in ballistic type movements as a part of their sport, e.g. Karate, may find it useful after appropriate warm up, and static stretching. However it is the riskiest and least effective form of stretching. PNF stretching is highly effective, but can be difficult to learn just from looking at pictures and reading descriptions. It is best if you're instructed in PNF techniques one-on-one. Each of the three basic methods has their benefits, but we're going to focus on the static stretching method because it has the least risk for injury and is the easiest to accomplish.

Static stretches are usually positions of stretch that are sustained for a period of time, to enable both the contractile and non-contractile elements of the muscle to adapt to the position. That means you need to stretch slowly, moving into position gently and holding the position for about 30 seconds. This will reduce the tendency to stimulate what is called the stretch reflex. The stretch reflex is a protective mechanism that reflexively contracts a muscle if it is rapidly stretched. Sustained stretching will avoid this reflex and allow the muscle to lengthen. A 1994 study in the journal Physical Therapy found that the optimum duration of stretch was approximately 30 seconds with no significant benefit to be had from holding it longer[1]. As far as how many repetitions to do of each stretch, a 1990 study in the American Journal of Sports Medicine reported that long lasting increases in flexibility could be achieved with 3-5 repetitions, with little benefit to be had from more repetitions[6]. With this in mind, regularly stretching each muscle group for 3 repetitions of about 30 seconds each should be sufficient.

To perform your stretches correctly, move slowly into the position until you feel a GENTLE "pulling sensation" in the muscle that is being stretched. As you hold this position, breathe and relax – focusing your attention on the muscle that is being stretched. ***Avoid the urge to "push it" to the limits.*** Simply feel a gentle pull and stay put. Stretching harder will tend to do more harm than good. More is not better in this case! Stretching more frequently throughout the day, or more consistently day after day, will buy you something. Stretching harder will not. Once adequate flexibility has been gained, studies show that it can be maintained with as little as one session per week.[7] But beware, when you stop stretching for a period of time, you will lose the flexibility you have worked so hard to gain.[8] Consistency is the key. For most athletes, stretching on a daily basis is best. Perform 2-3 repetitions of each stretch, holding the position for about 30 seconds.

What to stretch

Every individual is unique, with unique biomechanical, strength, occupational, and training characteristics. These unique characteristics determine what areas will need to be stretched. However, there are a few muscle groups that are so consistently tight on the majority of athletes that it is generally safe for all athletes to perform these stretches. Muscles of the calf, hamstrings, hip flexors and quadriceps fall into this category. There are numerous other muscle groups that could benefit from stretching , but this is a good beginning. Other stretches are presented following these first four key muscle groups. There are obviously other ways to stretch besides the techniques shown here, but these stretches are both safe and effective. A few rules of the road need to be reviewed here, then we'll move on to the specific stretching exercises.

RULES OF THE ROAD -

1. **Pain is <u>never</u> acceptable when stretching.** Stretching should be comfortable and relaxing, never painful. If something hurts, you're not in the right position or you've stretched too vigorously. Back off and check your position, then try again more gently.

2. **Slow and steady wins the race.** Slow movements into the position of stretch will avoid stimulating the stretch reflex, and will allow you

to tune into your muscle's signals. Don't rush it. Once in position, hold steady – no bouncing allowed.

3. **The position of stretch should generally be held for about 30 seconds.**

4. **The stretch should occur where indicated on the pictures.** If you're feeling it some other place, chances are you're not in the right position. Have a friend look at the picture and then look at you to see if you're in the correct position. There are subtle nuances to the instructions on each of the stretches; attention to these will generally put you in the correct position.

5. **Be consistent.** The more consistently you perform these stretches the more effective you will be in increasing your flexibility. Stretching daily initially and later 3 times a week for maintenance is a good rule of thumb.

Calf Muscle Stretch

Stand with your hands on a wall, and place one foot in front of the other as shown here. Put all your weight on the back foot. <u>Now for the</u> <u>important part</u>: ***Roll your back foot slightly to the outside to elevate your*** ***arch a little (see figure 1). Lift your toes a little to lock this position in***

Keep this knee straight & place all your weight into this heel

Feel stretch here

This knee bends & isn't holding much body weight

Lift big toe

Roll foot slightly to outside to lift the arch

place (see figure 2). Keep your heel down ***and your knee straight.*** Now slightly bend the forward knee, moving your hips toward the wall a little. Make sure to keep your hips right under your shoulders; don't stick your buttocks out! (See figure 2) You should begin to feel a GENTLE stretch or pulling sensation in the calf muscle of the back leg (the one with all the weight on it) - just below your knee. If you feel discomfort in the calf, arch of the foot, or knee **BACK OFF!** Don't stretch so hard. If you feel discomfort on the lateral side (outside) of your ankle, chances are you have rolled your foot too far to the outside. Try letting your

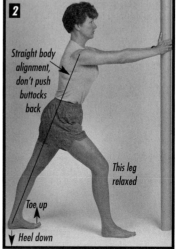

Straight body alignment, don't push buttocks back

This leg relaxed

Toe up

Heel down

foot back down a little. Hold this position of stretch for about 30 seconds, then switch legs and do the same procedure on the other side.

KEY POINTS:

1. All your body weight should be on the back foot.

2. Keep your heel down.

3. Lift your arch slightly and lock in place by lifting the toes.

4. The knee on the back leg should be straight.

5. Stretch only to the point of a pull — never pain. Hold for about 30 seconds.

Hamstring Stretch

Form is everything! Stand facing squarely toward a chair and make sure your hips, chest and both feet are all facing directly toward the chair. _Without turning your hips,_ place the heel of one foot up on the chair or low stool — **_keeping your knee _slightly_ bent (see arrow, figure 1)._** Now, without fully straightening your knee, try to pull your buttocks back and

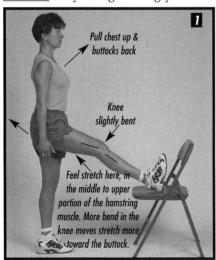

Pull chest up &
buttocks back

Knee
slightly bent

Feel stretch here, in
the middle to upper
portion of the hamstring
muscle. More bend in the
knee moves stretch more
toward the buttock.

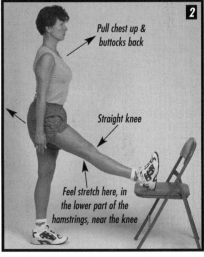

Pull chest up &
buttocks back

Straight knee

Feel stretch here, in
the lower part of the
hamstrings, near the knee

chest up at the same time (see arrows). This will put the axis of rotation at your hip joint rather than in your back. Make sure to **_avoid rounding your back._** You should feel a gentle pulling sensation or stretch in the back of the thigh of the leg that is up on the chair. If you feel _pain_ in the back of the thigh or in your lower back region, BACK OFF! Don't stretch so hard! If you can't accomplish this position with your foot on a chair, then use a step stool or stack of phone books. Hold the position for a gentle stretch of 30 seconds. Repeat the same procedure on the other side. Depending on where you are tight (upper versus lower hamstring) you may feel a more effective stretch with your knee straight (see figure 2).

KEY POINTS:

1. Hips should stay square to the chair; turning your hips as you put your foot up on the chair is cheating!

2. Keep the knee slightly bent throughout the stretch to focus the stretch on the mid to upper portion of the hamstring muscle. Straighten the knee fully to focus the stretch lower where the hamstring muscle inserts behind the knee.

3. Don't let your back "round" - you must pivot by pulling the buttocks back and chest up.

4. ___Never stretch to the point of pain!___ A gentle pull is all it takes.

5. To stretch the upper portion of the hamstrings at their attachment to the hips, bend the knee to about 35 degrees and put more emphasis on pulling the buttocks back. You should feel the stretch move from the middle of the back of the thigh, to the area where your leg meets your buttocks.

Hip Flexor Stretch

Start in a half-kneeling position, with one foot flat on the floor and the other knee directly under the hip. You may find it helpful to put a pillow under your knee if kneeling on the hard floor is uncomfortable for you. From this position, check your posture and make sure your back

Perform a pelvic tilt & keep abdominals tight

"Tuck your tail"

Shift weight forward if needed but don't lose your pelvic tilt

Feel stretch here

is absolutely straight, with your shoulders, hips and knees all aligned. Since one of the hip flexor muscles attaches to the spine, what you do with your low back affects how well you're able to stretch the hip flexors. Now *perform a pelvic tilt* as shown by the black arrows. To visualize this move, picture yourself "tucking your tail between your legs". If you do this correctly, you'll immediately feel a gentle pull or stretch in the front of the hip and thigh region of the leg you're kneeling on (see arrows). Breathe, relax, and hold the stretch. If you don't feel any pull at all then shift your weight slightly forward, but *keep your pelvic tilt.* If you feel pain anywhere, BACK OFF! Don't stretch so hard! Hold this position for about 30 seconds. Repeat the procedure on the other side.

KEY POINTS:

1. Posture is <u>everything</u> here! You must maintain your pelvic tilt in order to place the stretch on the hip flexor muscle and avoid placing undue stress on the lumbar spine.

2. By bending the forward knee and shifting your weight forward, you can increase the stretch, but it is much harder to hold proper pelvic position.

Quadriceps Stretch

Stand next to a wall or chair for balance. Make sure both feet are pointing straight ahead. Loop a towel around one ankle and grasp it with one hand. Pull up on the towel, bringing your heel up slightly toward your buttocks. **Stop when your knee is bent 90 degrees, so you can ad-**

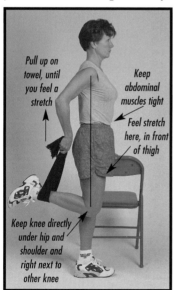

Pull up on towel, until you feel a stretch

Keep abdominal muscles tight

Feel stretch here, in front of thigh

Keep knee directly under hip and shoulder and right next to other knee

just your posture. Now, from this position, tighten your stomach muscles as if someone was about to punch you in the gut. This will keep your back from arching. Next, keeping your tummy tight, try to get your knee directly under your hip (see line in photo showing proper alignment). Now, *if you don't already feel a stretch in the muscle on the front of your thigh,* pull up <u>slightly</u> on the towel – drawing your heel a little closer to your buttocks (see arrow). You should feel a gentle pull in the muscle of the front of your thigh. If you feel **pain** in your back, or in the front of your thigh, BACK OFF! Don't stretch so hard! Posture is crucial here! If you lose your tummy muscle control, your back will arch and you'll lose the mechanical advantage to get the optimum stretch on the quadriceps muscle. The goal is not to get the heel to the buttocks, but rather to get the shoulders, hips and knees all in alignment. Hold the stretch for about 30 seconds. Repeat the procedure on the other side.

KEY POINTS:

1. Keep your stomach muscles tight throughout this exercise to insure that you aren't arching your back.

2. The goal is to get the knee directly under the hip, which is directly under the shoulder — *not* to get the foot to the buttocks.

3. Pull on the towel only until you feel a gentle stretch in the front of the thigh, if you feel pain you're stretching too hard.

4. If you are not feeling a stretch using a towel, try grasping the heel counter of your shoe with your index finger, but remember to keep your posture correct.

Adductor Stretch

To do this right, you need to sit with your buttocks and shoulders up against a wall. Sit on the floor, and scoot your buttocks back all the way until they contact the wall. Now place the soles of your feet together

Keep back & buttocks firmly pressed against wall

Let arms gently rest on knees, don't push

Feel stretch here

and draw them up slightly toward your groin. Rest your back and head and shoulders on the wall, using the wall to keep your back absolutely straight. There's no need to press down on your knees, just breathe, relax and let gravity draw them down toward the floor. Feel a gentle pull or stretch in the muscles of the inner thigh, from the groin area down toward the knee. If you feel *pain* in the groin area or anywhere else, BACK OFF! Don't stretch so hard! As this becomes easier, pull your feet up closer to your groin. Hold this position for about 30 seconds.

KEY POINTS:

1. In order to get the maximum benefit from this, you **must keep your buttocks and shoulders against the wall at all times**

2. Don't bounce; just let gravity do the work.

3. It isn't unusual to have one hip that's more flexible than the other, just keep working on this and listen to your body. Don't try to force the stretch.

4. There will be a tendency for your buttocks to slip away from the wall as you draw your feet toward your groin, double check your posture and adjust as needed.

Soleus Stretch

This calf stretch is for the powerful soleus muscle that lies underneath the gastrocnemius muscle in the lower part of your calf. Stand facing a table, counter or straight chair; about 6-12" back from the surface. Make sure both feet are pointing straight ahead. Place all your body weight on

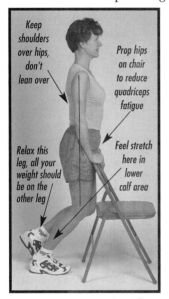

Keep shoulders over hips, don't lean over

Prop hips on chair to reduce quadriceps fatigue

Relax this leg, all your weight should be on the other leg

Feel stretch here in lower calf area

one leg, just resting the toes of the non-weight bearing leg lightly on the floor. Now *crouch slightly,* bending the knee of the weight bearing leg about 20 degrees. Next, bring your hips forward until they rest on the counter or back of the chair, making sure to *keep your back vertical and straight (see arrow in photo).* Let your hips prop firmly against the counter or chair, to take a little strain off the quadriceps muscle on the weight bearing leg. You should feel a *gentle* stretch or pulling sensation low in the calf muscle of the weight bearing leg. If you feel **pain** in the front of your ankle, or in the lower calf muscle, BACK OFF! Don't stretch so hard! If you don't feel a stretch at all, crouch a little lower. Hold the position about 30 seconds.

KEY POINTS:

1. Stay close to the table, counter or chair so that you can rest your hips on it and take the strain off your quadriceps muscle.

2. Make sure your toes are pointing straight ahead, don't toe out – that's cheating!

3. Crouch only slightly, and then bring your hips forward to rest on the chair.

4. NEVER stretch to the point of pain – only until you feel a gentle pull in the lower calf muscle. If you feel the stretch somewhere else, you're not in the right position

Iliotibial Band Stretch

The muscles on the outside of your hip act not only as powerful stabilizers as you run, they also assist the gluteals and hip flexors to move your leg forward and back. Tightness here can cause not only knee problems and back problems, but also can contribute to strains of other muscles in the area like the hamstrings. Likewise, tightness in the hamstrings and quadriceps can contribute to problems in the iliotibial band. (The IT band is often mistakenly labeled as the "perpetrator" when it is really a "victim" of lack of flexibility or lack of strength in its neighbors.)

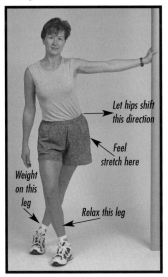

Let hips shift this direction

Feel stretch here

Weight on this leg

Relax this leg

To stretch the muscle that attaches to the iliotibial band effectively, stand about 18-24" away from a wall with your left side facing the wall. Place your hand on the wall at about shoulder height and then shift your weight so it is all being borne on the leg closest to the wall. Now, gently shift your hips toward the wall, *without moving your shoulders toward the wall.* The other leg should be relaxed, and if you're more comfortable placing it in front of the leg you're standing on that's fine. Just make sure it isn't bearing substantial weight. You should feel a GENTLE stretch on the outside of the hip that is closest to the wall. If you feel pain in your knee or anywhere else, BACK OFF!

Don't stretch so hard. You can adjust the position to achieve a stretch in different fibers of the muscle by *very slightly* bending the knee of the leg being stretched, or by slightly rotating your hips one-way or the other. Adjust it to see what works best for you. Hold the position for about 30 seconds.

KEY POINTS:

1. Make sure that as your hips move toward the wall, your shoulders remain stationary

2. Keep your weight shifted onto the leg being stretched (the one closest to the wall)

3. Adjust the position to stretch different fibers of the muscle group by slightly flexing the knee, or by rotating your hips slightly forward or backward.

4. The stretch should feel good, never painful and should be localized to the area shown

Spinal Rotation Stretch ("Rising Sun")

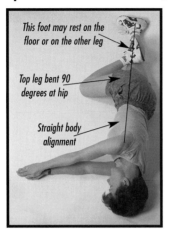

This foot may rest on the floor or on the other leg

Top leg bent 90 degrees at hip

Straight body alignment

Start from a *sidelying* position, with the top leg bent 90 degrees at the hip. Bend the knee to place the foot comfortably on the floor or tucked behind the other knee. Place both arms fully outstretched in front of you. Slowly lift the top hand, allowing the weight of this arm to rotate your body back. ***Keep your hips in the sidelying position, and try to keep your knee on the floor.*** Breathe, relax, and each time you exhale focus on letting your arm drop a little closer to the floor. Hold this position for about 30 seconds or 10 breaths. Slowly return to the start position (sidelying), then roll over and repeat the pro-

cedure on the other side. You may feel the stretch in any number of places – depending on where you're tight; the chest, shoulder, mid back, lower back, hip and thigh are all common areas. If you feel **pain** in your back or elsewhere, BACK OFF!

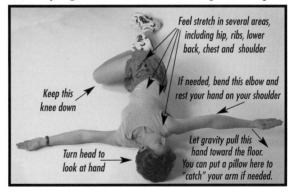

Feel stretch in several areas, including hip, ribs, lower back, chest and shoulder

If needed, bend this elbow and rest your hand on your shoulder

Keep this knee down

Let gravity pull this hand toward the floor. You can put a pillow here to "catch" your arm if needed.

Turn head to look at hand

Don't go so far. Repeat the stretch once or twice each side.

KEY POINTS:

1. Breathing is a crucial part of this exercise; let gravity do the work for you and focus on your breathing throughout.

2. Make sure to keep your hips in the sidelying position – it helps to hold your knee down if your hips tend to rotate back with your upper body.

3. *Always* start the exercise from the sidelying position.

4. Don't force the movement; let gravity do it for you.

5. If you feel like the stretch is too much, try bending your arm so that your fingertips rest on your shoulder. This will effectively shorten the lever that is rotating you back. Another option is to place a pillow on the floor to "catch" your arm as you rotate back so that you don't

rotate as far. Remember it should feel good, not painful.

6. To change the location of the stretch, change the arm position from straight out, to slightly overhead or slightly down toward the hip. Experiment a little to find what is most comfortable for you.

Gluteal Stretch

Tight gluteal muscles can contribute to a whole host of problems including low back pain, groin pain, iliotibial band syndrome, and knee pain among others. This is a nice relaxing stretch to do after a workout and cool down. Lie flat on a firm surface with both knees bent and feet flat on the floor. Cross one leg over the other, "guy-style", with the ankle resting on the knee of the other leg. Now bring the legs up toward your chest, grasping behind the knee of the crossed leg. You should feel a gentle pull in the buttock of the leg that is on top. In the photo, the stretch is being performed on the right leg. Keep your head and shoulders down and breathe and relax. If you

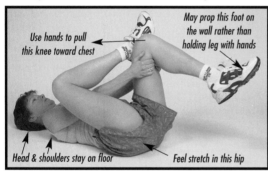

Use hands to pull this knee toward chest

May prop this foot on the wall rather than holding leg with hands

Head & shoulders stay on floor

Feel stretch in this hip

feel any *pain* in the hip or back, BACK OFF! Don't stretch so hard. If you are very tight in your hips, you may need to use a towel looped around behind your knee and grasp the towel to pull the legs up toward your chest. Another alternative is to prop the left foot on a wall when stretching the right hip, and the right foot on the wall when stretching the left hip. This position will allow you to maintain the stretch without having to hold your knee with your hands or a towel. Hold this position for about 30 seconds, and then do the same procedure on the other leg.

KEY POINTS:

1. Keep your head and shoulders down, and relax throughout the stretch.

2. Crossing your legs "guy-style" stretches one group of muscles; you can get another stretch by crossing "girl-style" (knee resting on knee, rather than ankle on knee).

3. Stretch only to the point of a pull never to the point of pain

Piriformis Stretch

The piriformis muscle is one of a group of small but powerful muscles deep in your buttocks whose primary role is to act as external rotators of your hip. Because of its angle of pull, it is one of the muscles that act as a strong decelerator of pronation. Since the muscle attaches to the front of your sacral bone (a triangular shaped bone at the base of your spine) this insures that it can have a powerful impact on the dynamics of joints both above it and below it. Lack of adequate flexibility in this muscle can contribute to lower back pain, as well as problems in the hips and knees. To do this stretch, lie flat on your back and place the heel of one foot on

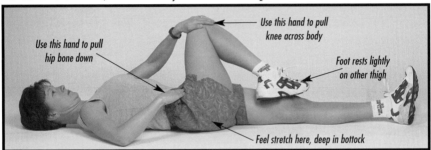

Use this hand to pull knee across body

Use this hand to pull hip bone down

Foot rests lightly on other thigh

Feel stretch here, deep in bottock

the top of the opposite knee. Grasp your knee with the opposite hand and gently pull your knee across your body – making sure to keep your hips flat on the floor. Done correctly, you'll feel a gentle stretch or pull deep in the buttock region. If you feel discomfort or "pinching" in the groin area, try repositioning your leg a little lower, with the heel resting just below the other knee. Keep your head and shoulders down. Breathe, relax, and hold the stretch for about 30 seconds. If you feel *pain* in your back or elsewhere, BACK OFF! Don't stretch so hard. Return to the starting position and repeat the procedure on the other side.

KEY POINTS:

1. Keep your hips, shoulders and head resting comfortably on the floor throughout the stretch, hold the hip down with your hand if needed.

2. Adjust the position of your foot if you feel a pinching sensation in the groin area. Sliding the foot slightly down the leg usually works, but you may need to bring it up the thigh a little further. Experiment and find the position that is most comfortable for you.

3. Breathe and relax, let the weight of your hand provide the force.

4. The only place you should feel the stretch is in the hip/buttock region.

Spinal Flexion And Extension Stretch

Start in hands and knees position ("all fours"). Make sure your hands

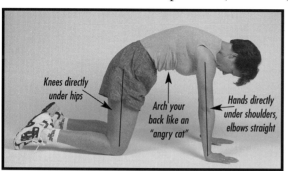

are right under your shoulders and your knees are right under your hips. Next, tighten your tummy muscles and tuck your tail, arching your back up like an angry cat (see left photo). Hold this position *briefly,* about 3-5 seconds. Then sag your back down and stick your buttocks up, like an

old horse (see right photo). You shouldn't feel any discomfort in either direction, if you do BACK OFF! Don't go quite so far in the motions. Repeat this cycle, arching and then sagging, about 10 times holding each position for about 3-5 seconds.

KEY POINTS:

1. The movement should all come from your back, ***don't let your elbows flex and extend.*** This isn't a push-up!

2. Hips should stay right over your knees, and shoulders right over your wrists throughout the movement.

3. All movements should be comfortable; you should never feel pain in your back or legs.

4. The movement is a rhythmic one, no need to hold for sustained stretch as in other stretches.

REFERENCES CHAPTER THREE

1. Bandy WD, Irion JM. *The effect of time of static stretch on the flexibility of the hamstring muscles.* Phys Ther 74: 845-850, 1994.

2. Davis VB. *Flexibility conditioning for running.* In D'Ambrosia RD, Drez D (eds): Prevention and Treatment of Running Injuries, 2nd ed. Thorofare, NJ, Slack, 1989, pp. 221-231.

3. Malone TR, Garrett WE Jr., Zachazewski JE. *Muscle: Deformation, injury, repair.* In Zachazewski JE, Magee DJ, Quillen WS (eds): Athletic Injuries and Rehabilitation. WB Saunders, Philadelphia, 1996, pp. 71-91.

4. Safran MR, Garrett WE, Seaber AV, et al. *The role of warm-up in muscular injury prevention.* Am J Sports Med 16: 123-129, 1988.

5. Simoneau GG, Wilk KE, Clancy WG Jr. *Strengthening and Flexibility Concepts for Runners.* In Guten GN (ed) Running Injuries. WB Saunders, Philadelphia, 1997, pp. 238-253.

6. Taylor DC, Dalton JD Jr., Seaber AV, Garrett WE Jr. *Viscoelastic properties of muscle-tendon units: The biomechanical effects of stretching.* Am J Sports Med 18:300-309, 1990.

7. Wallin D, Ekblom B, Grahn R, Nordenborg T. *Improvement of muscle flexibility: A comparison between two techniques.* Am J Sports Med 13:263-268, 1985.

8. Zebas CJ, Rivera ML. *Retention of flexibility in selected joints after cessation of a stretching exercise program.* In Dotson CE, Humphrey JH (eds) Exercise Physiology: Current selected research. New York, AMS Press, 1985.

CHAPTER FOUR

STRENGTH

Components of strength

Strength consists of elements of power, endurance, and balance/control (otherwise known as proprioception). A good example of the interaction of these elements would be an elite figure skater, who must have explosive power to jump, endurance to maintain speed and power throughout a long program, and exceptional proprioception (balance and control) to land jumps successfully. Each athletic pursuit has its own combination of requirements, some having a greater requirement for muscular endurance and stamina, others having a greater requirement for explosive power. Knowing your sport and understanding it's requirements will help you to prioritize your training.

Specificity

It all starts with knowing what you want to accomplish and then working backwards to figure out how to get there. Specificity means that being a fabulous swimmer doesn't necessarily make you a great cyclist. Likewise running many miles doesn't insure that you'll be a good swimmer. To gain the right kind of strength, you must be specific in your training demands. That isn't to say that there isn't a place for cross training. On the contrary, when you're fighting an injury cross training can be your best road to recovery.

Why strength train?

Since your muscles are the chief shock absorber in your body, their strength plays a critical role in injury prevention[2]. The altered function of these shock absorbers due to fatigue on a long training run is one of the main factors associated with stress fractures and other overuse injuries[3]. Though running may not make you a better weight lifter, it is clear that strength training can make you a better runner.

What to train?

Well, that depends on the activity in which you want to ultimately excel, and what injuries you're trying to avoid or rehabilitate. If basketball is your chosen sport, you'll need massive power in your gluteals, quads and hamstrings to give you the needed height on your vertical jump. On the other hand, if you're training to run marathons raw power isn't as important as stamina. The first step is to decide what is your goal. Will you be running or walking? Will the distances be short (sprints of 400 - 800 meters or less), medium (one mile to 5K), long (10K to marathon) or ultra distance (> marathon)? Will you be competing in multi-sport events (duathlons, triathlons, etc)? Are you training for a specific event, i.e. an upcoming ski trip or mountain climbing? The answers to each of these questions will lead you generally to the type of training that is appropriate for you. Generally the shorter the duration of the activity (sprints, team sports) the more the emphasis will be on explosive power. The longer duration events call for a greater focus on balancing muscle strength and on increasing stamina. If power is the focus, fewer repetitions with a greater amount of resistance will generally achieve optimum strength and this can be followed by more intense exercises like plyometrics (jumping drills, etc). If the focus is more on endurance, as in the case of middle and long distance running and walking events, a greater number of repetitions with relatively less resistance will be the most effective means of gaining the appropriate strength.

How to train?

There are dozens of equipment makers that will tell you that their latest model of the "X" machine is the greatest. However, you can do quite well in most cases with body weight, gravity, four walls and a floor. Occasionally it helps to have some hand weights or elastic bands to offer additional resistance, but membership at a gym is not required to maximize your benefits. Generally when training for power or strength, using free weights rather than machines is more effective. Using free weights requires that you both lift *and control* the weight. It means that you must contract synergistic muscles to make sure that you accomplish the movement in the right fashion. This way, you train not only the prime movers, but also the muscles that help to give you controlled, quality movement. A good example of this is the use of free weights to do a squat, versus

○ *Generally when training for power or strength, using free weights rather than machines is more effective. Using free weights requires that you both lift and control the weight.*

using a leg press machine. When doing squats, you must balance the weight appropriately at the start of the exercise and then continuously adjust your balance as your body moves through space and your center of gravity moves. On the other hand when you sit in a leg press machine (or lie on the inverted style ones), you don't have to balance a thing – just push against the machine and it will maintain the proper alignment because it is designed to do just that. You may gain strength from this exercise, but you'll not gain the same amount of control, balance and power as you would if you spent the same amount of time doing a free weight exercise like a squat. With that said, it is sometimes better to use machines for strength training. Instances where this comes to mind include individuals who have a compromised sense of balance, and individuals who are recovering from a traumatic injury and must avoid certain motions or firing certain muscles. Generally even if you've never lifted weights before, you can learn to perform free-weight exercises[1]. After all, your body is a free weight and you seem to handle it pretty well don't you?

When to train?

There is no one "best" time of day to strength train. Work it into your schedule as it suits you. There are however ways of cycling your training that can prove beneficial. Think of the professional sports teams - they have an off-season as well as a competitive season. The majority of the strength building is done in the off-season and early pre-season, skill building and other things are emphasized as the competitive season approaches. Following this same theory, runners and walkers would do well to cycle their training somewhat. Choose a couple of events in which you'd like to do really well and cycle your training so that you have a rest season right after a racing season, and a strength and base building season well before the racing season. A speed building or "sharpening" season would occur as the racing season nears. The choice of when during your training week to do strength training is highly individual. Some like to do their strength training workouts on their "easy" mileage days, others like to do it on the "medium" mileage days. What ever works best for you is fine. It would be best to avoid strength training on long mileage days or on days in which you will be doing speedwork.

> ➊ *Choose a couple of events in which you'd like to do really well and cycle your training so that you have a rest season right after a racing season, and a strength and base building season well before the racing season. A speed building or "sharpening" season would occur as the racing season nears.*

Reps, sets and such

A "rep" is one repetition of a motion – one squat, one lunge, one bench press. A "set" is a group of repetitions of an exercise, for example one set of 10 repetitions, one set of 15 repetitions, etc. Multiple sets are often performed, separated by a rest break. For example, to do 3 sets of 15 reps of squats, you would perform the first set of 15 reps and then rest for a brief period (60 seconds or so) before doing the second set, and rest again before the third set. Another way to stimulate the cardiac benefit and improve your stamina is to pedal a stationary bike or jump rope or bench step between exercises. This form of exercise, where you do not fully rest between sets is often called "circuit training" or "aerobic circuit training". The benefit is that you work on both muscular strength/endurance and cardiovascular conditioning at the same time.

Increasing the intensity

There are a myriad of ways to make an exercise harder, depending on the exercise and the equipment (if any) you're using. You can increase the difficulty by lifting more weight, or changing the speed of the exercise, or increasing the range of motion. If you're using free weights or machines, it is best to increase the resistance by the smallest possible increment. In some cases this may be a 10-pound increase, in others it may be as little as 3 pounds. Regardless, you want to make the changes gradually. Only increase the resistance when you can easily accomplish the specified reps and sets of the exercise feeling only minimally taxed at the end. If you're struggling at all with the current weight, don't increase it. Increasing the resistance each work out is a very bad idea and will surely put you at greater risk of injury. Give yourself at least 4-6 workouts at a specified resistance before even thinking about increasing it. For exercises done with body weight only, sometimes increasing the range of motion will be enough to make the exercise harder. For example, if you've been doing one-quarter depth squats, try squatting to chair height (half-depth). If you've been doing balance and reach exercises, reach farther. Sometimes simply doing a balance and reach exercise with your eyes closed is a good way to challenge yourself.

What will I feel the next day?

Initially, strength training will give most people at least some degree of delayed onset muscle soreness. This occurs in most people within 48 hours of performing the strength training work out. This is one good reason to start slowly – do less than you think you are able to the first few workouts. You'll be surprised at just how little it takes of some exercises to bring on the soreness, so proceed with caution.

Contrary to popular wisdom, the soreness is not a result of lactic acid in your muscles; it is instead a result of micro-trauma to the muscles and indicates that you probably pushed your limits a bit. Generally this soreness can be classified as follows: "Acceptable" – a mild sense of soreness with some movements (like getting up/down from toilet, in/out of car etc.) but just walking around isn't painful. "Pushing it" – noticeably sore with most movements, including just walking around. "Overdoing it" – lying in bed and turning over hurts. Generally if you can keep your soreness at the "acceptable" level or less, and you're not feeling any joint pain, you're doing OK. If you're feeling more pain in the joints than the muscles, or if you're "pushing it" or "overdoing it" - you need to back off and take several days rest before trying again. Strength training stimulates muscles to get stronger by pushing them to their limits. If you consistently push beyond those limits, you run the risk of causing an injury. Do not to get into the "No pain, No gain" syndrome, that will surely get you into trouble.

> ❍ *Strength training stimulates muscles to get stronger by pushing them to their limits. If you consistently push beyond those limits, you run the risk of causing an injury. Do not to get into the "No pain, No gain" syndrome, that will surely get you into trouble.*

When in doubt...

Do less. Listen to your body; pain is the universal signal that something is wrong. If you're having pain in your joints, either the exercise is too advanced for you or you're increasing the intensity too fast, or your form is off. If you're new to strength training, take it slowly and focus on technique first. The exercises described in the following pages may look easy on paper, but they can be quite intense so it is best to start slowly.

RULES OF THE ROAD ----------------------------------

1. Pain is never acceptable when strength training. You should clearly "feel" your muscles working as you perform the exercises, and you may feel fatigue and even "heavy legs" for a few days after, but pain should never be an issue. If something hurts, you're either doing too much too soon, or your form is incorrect. Back off and take a few days off, then resume again but at a lower level of intensity.

2. Slow and steady wins the race. Generally movements should be rhythmic and steady and progressions of intensity or repetitions should be gradual over a period of several weeks.

3. Form is crucial. Have a friend look at the picture and then look at you to see if you're in the correct position. There are subtle nuances to the instructions on each of the exercises; attention to these will generally put you in the correct position.

4. Be consistent. Strength training with body weight resistance as shown here can be done daily without risking injury once you have gained enough strength. Initially performing these exercises 3-4 times a week will prove challenging. Once adequate strength is gained, you can reduce the frequency of training to 2-3 times a week and not risk losing your hard-earned gains.

5. Strength training is best done on days other than your extra long or speed-work days. ▰▰▰▰▰▰▰▰▰▰▰▰▰▰▰▰▰▰▰▰▰▰▰▰▰▰▰

ORDER OF ATTACK

The exercises are presented in order from the easiest to the more challenging, however each exercise presented has variables that can be modified to make it relatively easier or harder. A general rule of thumb is: any exercise that is performed in static weight bearing position (the squat for example) is easier than one in which there is dynamic movement (such as lunges). Likewise any exercise which requires you to balance while moving (such as the balance and reach exercises) is more challenging than those that do not challenge the body's sense of balance as much (such as the lunges). A summary is presented at the end of the chapter, to help the reader determine a reasonable order of progression on the exercises.

Squats

Probably the most functional exercise you'll ever learn, the squat is a basic fundamental movement that you repeat numerous times throughout the day. Every time you sit in a chair, you performed a squat to get there. Every time you get up, you get up from a squat. This exercise also teaches the basic movement for safe lifting mechanics. Utilizing the body mechanics shown in the photo, you keep your back in a position of safety and use the large muscles of your buttocks and thighs to accomplish the task at hand. Start this exercise standing with your feet a shoulder's width apart; toes pointing ahead or very slightly turned out (see figure 2). Tighten your tummy muscles slightly and then place your hands on your hips, to remind you that you're to pivot from the hips not the back. Keeping your back straight but NOT vertical, squat down as if you were going to sit on a chair but you didn't know how low it was. As you squat, your chest should be over your knees, which are over your feet – making

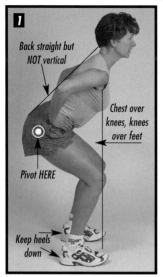

1

Back straight but NOT vertical

Chest over knees, knees over feet

Pivot HERE

Keep heels down

your center of gravity very stable and centered over your feet (see figure 1). If you feel yourself falling backwards, you're not pivoting from the hips – bring your chest more over your knees.

Your knees should track straight over your feet; don't let them fall in toward each other (see figure 2).

You should eventually be able to squat to chair height without lifting your heels off the ground.

Once you're accustomed to the movement, try folding your arms across your chest or placing your hands clasped behind your neck. This will change your center of gravity a little and force you to pivot from the hips.

It helps to do this exercise in front of a full-length mirror to check your form, or have a partner look at this picture and check your form. Proper form is crucial. How low you squat depends on how well you can maintain form, your ankle flexibility and several other factors. Depth is not the primary issue here, form is. Squat only to a depth that is comfortable for you, there is rarely a need to squat to a depth where your buttocks are below knee height. You should be able to maintain good form throughout the movement. If you're unsure of yourself, place a chair behind you and squat until your buttocks

2

Knees should track straight over feet. Don't let them come in toward each other.

Feet straight ahead

just barely brush the edge of the chair seat. This will give you a "target" to aim for. Don't hold the position, just squat down and then return to the starting position. If you feel pain anywhere, don't squat so low!

KEY POINTS

1. Feet should be a shoulder width apart - toes facing straight ahead or slightly toed out.

2. Keep your back straight but not vertical, it helps to think "stick your buttocks back" and "keep your chest over your knees".

3. Keep both heels on the ground, this makes sure that your base of support is stable and encourages you to pivot from the hips.

4. Make sure that your knees track straight over your feet and don't fall toward each other as you squat.

5. Squat only as deep as you can go without losing your good form. Most people can eventually squat to chair seat height with good form. Some can eventually maintain good form even deeper than that, but there is rarely a need to perform squats to depths where your buttocks are below knee height. Depth is not the issue – form is.

6. If you feel pain in your knee joints, don't squat so low – keep the movement pain free. You should feel your thigh muscles and buttock muscles working, but you should not have any joint pain anywhere. If you're having back pain as you do this movement, your form is incorrect; squat to a shallower depth and work on keeping your back straight but chest over knees. Remembering to tighten your tummy muscles before you start the movement will also help.

7. To increase the intensity of the exercise, try holding a broomstick across your shoulders, behind your head. Another way to make it more difficult is to hold small hand weights, or use a light barbell in place of the broomstick. Varying the speed of the squat - sometimes going faster or slower will also change the intensity of the exercise.

8. Obviously, squatting to deeper depths also makes it more intense – but you've got to maintain form.

MUSCLES WORKED

Gluteals – the "seat of your power"...your buttocks.

Hamstrings – the back of the thigh

Quadriceps – the front of the thigh

Adductors – the inner thigh

Abdominals – the tummy

Spinal extensors – the lower back

Forward lunge

This exercise is great for building hamstring, quadriceps and gluteal strength, as well as stimulating your sense of balance. It is also a good *dynamic* stretch for the quadriceps, soleus, and hip flexor muscles. Start

Back straight & nearly vertical

Knee doesn't extend past toe

Bend this knee

Take a big step

by standing straight, both feet facing straight ahead. Tighten your tummy muscles and then take a big step forward with one foot. Land heel first, like you would normally, and as your weight shifts forward onto this leg bend your knee to absorb the shock a little. Lunge forward as shown in figure 1, making sure to keep your heel down on the floor. Allow the back leg to bend a little at the knee and the heel of that foot should naturally roll up off the ground as your weight shifts forward onto the lunging leg. Keep your back straight and mostly vertical, never leaning any further forward than shown in figure 1. Your chest should NOT be over your knee, rather over your hips. Make sure to keep your knee tracking straight over your foot; don't let it fall to the inside (see figure 2). Do not hold this position, simply lunge and then immediately push back up to return to the starting position. Lunge only as far as you are able to get back to the starting position with one push. Taking little hops to return to the start position means you stepped out too far. It isn't important that your back knee touches the floor – the depth of the lunge will depend on many factors including your hip strength, your ankle flexibility, and your balance. Depth isn't the issue here, form is. To promote stamina, do all repetitions on one leg before changing to the other side. If

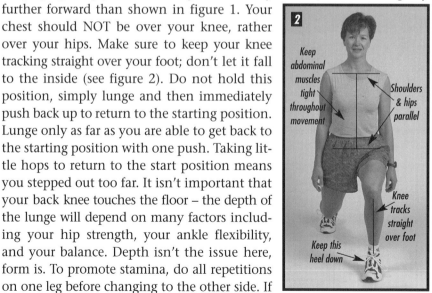

Keep abdominal muscles tight throughout movement

Shoulders & hips parallel

Knee tracks straight over foot

Keep this heel down

you feel pain in your knees or anywhere else, BACK OFF! Don't step so far, or lunge so deep! You should feel the muscles of your buttocks and legs working, but it should not be painful.

KEY POINTS

1. Take as big a step as you can, without losing your balance or making it so that you can't return to the starting position with one push.

2. Keep the heel of the lunging foot on the ground, this will insure a better base of support and keep you from lunging so far that your knee gets in front of your foot.

3. Make sure that as you lunge you maintain good alignment of your knee, hip and foot. Don't let the knee fall to the inside as you lunge.

4. To build stamina, perform all repetitions on one leg before switching to the other leg.

5. To increase intensity of the exercise, lunge farther or deeper – as long as you can maintain good form. Another way to increase the difficulty is to hold a broomstick on your shoulders behind your head, or hold small hand weights in your hands. Lunging in a "progressive" fashion, in other words coming up over the front leg rather than pushing back to "home base" will work the hamstrings a bit more. This can be done in alternating fashion, first lunging on the right and coming up over the right foot, then lunging on the left and coming up over the left foot. Varying the speed of the lunge can also provide additional challenge, but remember form is everything!

6. If you feel pain in your knee joints or anywhere else, you're lunging too far or too deep for your capabilities. The exercise should be pain free.

MUSCLES WORKED

Gluteals - the "seat" of your power, your buttocks

Hamstrings - the back of the thigh (especially with "progressive" lunges)

Quadriceps - the front of the thigh

Adductors - the inner thigh

Abdominals and spinal extensors - tummy and lower back

Lateral lunge

This is a good exercise to strengthen your inner and outer thighs as well as your buttocks. These muscles are often neglected in the standard strengthening exercises so this particular exercise helps fill a major void. Start from a standing position, with feet together. Take a big step to the side with one foot, and as your weight shifts onto that foot, bend your

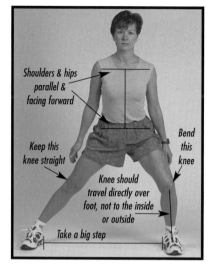

Shoulders & hips parallel & facing forward

Keep this knee straight

Knee should travel directly over foot, not to the inside or outside

Take a big step

Bend this knee

knee and lunge to the side. Make sure to keep your shoulders and hips parallel and facing squarely ahead. The leg that is stationary (back at home base) should remain straight, not flexing at the knee. Don't hold this position, simply lunge and then push off to return to the starting position. Take as large a step as you are able to, making sure that you're able to return to the starting position with one push. Multiple hops to return to the start position means you took too large a step. How deep you lunge is not important and will depend in part on your muscle strength, the condition of your knee joints, flexibility in your ankles, and sense of balance. Depth is not the issue here, form is. Make sure to maintain good posture throughout the exercise, and keep your feet parallel to each other and facing straight ahead at all times. Avoid the urge to toe out excessively on the lunging leg. To work on stamina, do all the repetitions on one leg before you switch and repeat the process on the other side. If you feel any pain in your knee joints or anywhere else, don't step so far or lunge so deep! The exercise should always be pain free.

KEY POINTS

1. Make sure your feet are parallel at all times and facing straight ahead.

2. Take as big a step as you can, but make sure you're able to get back to the starting position with just one push. If you have to hop back to the start position, you took too big a step.

3. Keep your shoulders and hips level and squarely facing forward.

4. To increase the intensity of the exercise, try holding a broomstick on your shoulders behind your head or hold some light hand weights in your hands. Stepping further and lunging deeper also make this exercise more intense, but make sure that you're not losing your good form or causing any discomfort when you do this. Varying the speed will change the dynamics of the exercise and may offer another challenge.

5. The exercise is to be pain free, if you're experiencing discomfort anywhere check your form. Shorter steps and shallower depths usually take care of the problem. You should feel the muscles in your hips and thighs working, but you shouldn't feel any pain.

> **MUSCLES WORKED**
>
> **Adductors** – inner thigh
>
> **Abductors** – outer thigh and hip
>
> **Gluteals** – the "seat" of your power, your buttocks
>
> **Hamstrings** – back of thigh
>
> **Quadriceps** – front of thigh
>
> **Abdominals and spinal extensors** – tummy and low back

Lateral rotational lunge

This variant of the lateral lunge adds the element of rotation to the mix, making it a bit more challenging than the straight lateral lunge. The focus here is on keeping the body and lunging foot moving one direction, while keeping the stationary leg firmly fixed and facing in the original direction. Start this exercise standing with your feet together, toes point-

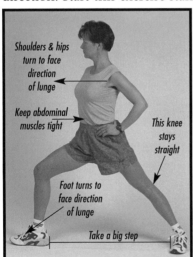

Shoulders & hips turn to face direction of lunge

Keep abdominal muscles tight

This knee stays straight

Foot turns to face direction of lunge

Take a big step

ing straight ahead. Take a big step to the side with one foot, simultaneously turning your foot and your body to face the direction you just stepped. This position is reminiscent of a "fencing" lunge. Land heel first, as you would normally, and then as your foot comes into contact with the ground bend your knee and lunge. Note that the stationary leg does not bend – the knee is straight. Do not hold this position, simply lunge and then push off to return to the start position, making sure that as you return you _rotate back to a forward facing position._

How deep you lunge isn't important – how well you rotate and how big a step you take are the key issues here. Form is all-important! You must be able to get back to the starting position with one push, if you have to take little hops then you took too big a step. If you feel any pain in your knees, hips, back, or anywhere else, don't step so far or lunge so deep! To build stamina, do all your repetitions on one leg before repeating the procedure going the opposite direction.

KEY POINTS:

1. Start with both feet facing the same direction; keep the stationary foot facing this direction throughout the exercise.

2. Rotate your body and your lunging foot to face the direction you're lunging. The lunging knee bends, the stationary one does not.

3. Take a big step, but not so big that you can't get back to the start position with one push. Depth is variable, depending on the condition of your knee and hip joints, your muscle flexibility and strength, and your sense of balance.

4. Make sure that you rotate back to straight ahead when you return to the start position each repetition. This keeps the rotational element in the exercise for subsequent repetitions.

5. To increase the intensity of the exercise, try holding a broomstick on your shoulders behind your head, or hold some light hand weights in your hands. Also increasing the step length or lunge depth will increase the difficulty. You can also vary the speed a little from slower to faster repetitions.

6. You should never feel pain with this or any other exercise. You may feel the muscles of your hips and thighs working, but if you're having pain in the knee or hip joints (or anywhere else) you need to check your form and maybe back off a bit. Try shortening the step length and not lunging as deep. If this doesn't resolve the discomfort, you're probably not ready for this exercise.

MUSCLES WORKED:

Gluteals and deep hip rotators – the "seat" of your power, your buttocks

Hamstrings – back of thigh

Adductors – inner thigh

Quadriceps – front of thigh

Abdominals and spinal extensors – tummy and lower back

Posterior-lateral balance and reach

This backward (posterior) and diagonal reach is a great way to really fire up your gluteal muscles and hamstrings. Like all balance and reach exercises the rules are simple: you balance on one leg and then reach *but don't touch.* By holding your balance on one leg while you dynamically move your other leg, you challenge your body's intricate balance system at the same time you're challenging your muscles to get stronger. You get a lot of bang for the buck here. Start by standing straight, with

Hands behind back like a speed skater

Feel it working here

Reach back but don't touch

Knee nicely lined up over foot

your arms tucked behind your back like a speed skater. Make sure both feet are facing straight ahead. Now, balance on your left leg and reach your right leg back and diagonally to your left. Try to keep your foot within one inch of the floor, but don't touch – that's cheating. Your goal is to reach as far back along that line as you can, stretching your knee straight to maximize the reach. Don't hold the position, just reach and then return to the full upright standing start position and then repeat. To stimulate more stamina, do all your reps on one leg before

switching and repeating the process on the other side. Reach only as far as you're able to go without touching your foot down to the floor for balance. You should never feel pain with this exercise; you may well feel the muscles of your buttocks and legs working very hard though. If you feel pain in the knees, back or anywhere else, don't reach so far.

KEY POINTS:

1. For maximum challenge keep your hands behind your back, and don't touch your foot to the floor. If you're having trouble with your balance though, it's OK to "cheat" by holding your arms out to the side, until you get stronger. If you're really having trouble, you can hold the wall for balance or use a chair back for support – but the goal is to eventually do it with no assistance.

2. Keep your back straight throughout the movement, pivot from the hip rather than the spine.

3. The farther you reach, the more challenging the exercise – go as far as you can without pain or losing your balance.

> **MUSCLES WORKED:**
>
> **Gluteals (buttocks)** – the seat of your power
>
> **Abductors** – outsides of your hips
>
> **Hamstrings** – back of thigh
>
> **Quadriceps** – front of thigh
>
> **Spinal extensors** – lower and mid back region primarily

Balance and anterior reach with leg

This forward (anterior) reach is a great way to really fire up your quadri-

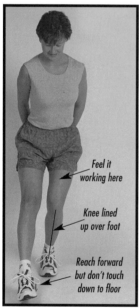

Feel it working here

Knee lined up over foot

Reach forward but don't touch down to floor

ceps and calf muscles. Like all balance and reach exercises the rules are simple: you balance on one leg and then reach but don't touch. By holding your balance on one leg while you dynamically move your other leg, you challenge your body's intricate balance system at the same time you're challenging your muscles to get stronger. These balance and reach exercises are intense. Start by standing straight, with your arms tucked behind your back like a speed skater. Make sure both feet are facing straight ahead. Now, balance on your left leg and reach your right leg forward. Try to keep your foot within one inch of the floor, but don't touch

Keep heel down

Reach but don't touch

– that's cheating. Reach as far forward along that line as you can, making sure to keep the left heel down on the floor. You should feel the muscles in the front of your thigh working, as well as your calf muscles, but you should never experience pain in the knee joint or anywhere else. Make sure to keep your knee tracking straight toward your foot; don't let it fall to the inside as it bends. If you're having pain, BACK OFF! Don't reach so far! Don't hold the position, simply reach as far as you can without losing your balance and then return to the starting position. To stimulate stamina, do all the repetitions on one leg before switching sides and repeating the process on the other leg.

KEY POINTS:

1. For maximum challenge keep your hands behind your back, and don't touch your foot to the floor. If you're having trouble with your balance though, it's OK to "cheat" and hold your hands out to the side, until you get stronger. If you're really having trouble, you can hold the wall for balance or use a chair back for support – but the goal is to eventually do it with no assistance.

2. Keep your heel down on the floor to maximize your base of support and to challenge both your ankle flexibility and strength.

3. The farther you reach, the more challenging the exercise – go as far as you can without pain or losing your balance.

4. If you have trouble with knee pain on this exercise, you're probably not ready for it. You'd be better off going back to the squats and lunges until you've built a little more strength. This exercise (like all of the balance and reach exercises) can be pretty intense. It is important to remember that NO EXERCISE should cause you pain.

MUSCLES WORKED:

Quadriceps – front of thigh

Gastrocnemius and soleus muscles – the calf muscle group

Foot intrinsic muscles – those small muscles in the foot that help you to grip with your toes

---

Balance and forward/diagonal reach with arm

This exercise strengthens your hamstrings, gluteal muscles and spinal extensors – as well as provides a great challenge to improve your proprioception. Start from a standing position, and place your left hand behind your back like a speed skater. Balance on your left leg, and lift your right leg slightly off the floor, making sure to keep it right next to the left leg. Now, reach down and forward with your right hand toward an imaginary target on the floor that is in front and slightly to the left. If you were reaching along compass points, you'd be reaching northwest with your right hand. Keep your right leg tucked in next to your left leg while you do this – using it as a counterbalance is cheating! Make sure to keep your left heel down on the floor as you reach forward; bending the left knee

Rest hand behind back

Reach diagonally in front of you, but don't touch

Keep this foot off the floor but right next to the other leg

OK to bend this knee, but keep heel down

is OK. You should feel your hamstrings and buttock muscles working, but it shouldn't be painful. If you're having pain, don't reach so far forward and try putting a chair in front of you and using the chair seat as a target to reach for rather than reaching all the way down to the floor. This exercise, which combines flexion and rotation, can be very challenging to your muscles and to your sense of balance! Don't hold the position, just reach and then return to an upright posture. Your goal is to accomplish all your repetitions without touching the non-weight bearing foot to the floor for balance. Remember, it should never ever be painful to do this – if it is you're going too far, or you're not ready for this exercise! For building stamina, do all your repetitions on one leg before switching and repeating this on the other side. Remember when you switch legs, you switch arms too!

KEY POINTS

1. The goal is to balance and reach – but don't touch!

2. Keep the non-weight bearing leg right next to the leg you're balancing on at all times – counterbalancing is cheating!

3. Keep your non-reaching arm tucked behind your back.

4. Keep the heel down and bend your knee as much as you like to enable you to reach forward and down.

5. Don't hold the position, just reach and then return to a full upright position.

6. The target is in front and off to the side, making you rotate a little. Place the "target" at an appropriate height – on the floor is the most challenging, a chair seat is an intermediate challenge, and the chair back would be the easiest. Make sure to choose a target distance and height that allows you to return smoothly to your start position without loosing your balance or form. *__It is better to start conservatively on this, and all, balance and reach exercises.__*

7. The exercise should never be painful – challenging yes, but painful – NO!!

> **MUSCLES WORKED:**
>
> **Hamstrings** – back of thigh
>
> **Gluteals** – the seat of your power, your buttocks
>
> **Quadriceps** – front of thigh
>
> **Spinal extensors** – your lower and mid back region particularly

CORE STRENGTH

No chapter on strength training would be complete without some focus on "core" strength. The abdominal muscles and spinal muscles form the "core" of stability so that force generated by the legs can be transferred into useful motion. Weakness of the abdominal and spinal muscles can play a role in many lower back and hip injuries. **As with the exercises shown for the lower extremities, these exercises, which focus on back and abdominal muscles, should not be performed if you are currently injured. It is always best to check with your health care provider to see which, if any, of these exercises are appropriate for you.** The exercises shown here will help you to develop the abdominal and back muscle strength that can help you avoid injury.

Let's start with the abdominal muscles.

Abdominal Stabilization Progression

This progression of abdominal exercises is part of a much larger series of exercises that are frequently

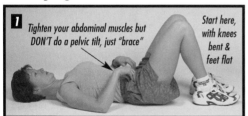

1 Tighten your abdominal muscles but DON'T do a pelvic tilt, just "brace"

Start here, with knees bent & feet flat

taught to individuals with lower back pain. Rather than present the entire series from the simplest to the most difficult, only a couple of the relatively more advanced exercises are presented here. The key to each of these exercises is maintaining stability in your mid section while you move your extremities. This is not done from a position of pelvic tilt (pushing your low back into the floor), but rather from a position of pelvic neutral (neither "swaybacked" or flat-backed).

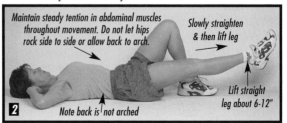

Maintain steady tention in abdominal muscles throughout movement. Do not let hips rock side to side or allow back to arch.

Slowly straighten & then lift leg

Lift straight leg about 6-12"

2 Note back is not arched

Lie on your back with both knees bent and feet flat on the floor. The beginning progression is shown in figures 1 and 2. First, place your hands behind your head and tighten your abdominal muscles so that your hips remain stable on the floor and your back doesn't arch or flatten as you move your extremities. While maintaining the tension in your abdominal muscles, straighten one leg, and then lift this straight leg up until the heel is 6-12 inches off the floor. Keep your tummy muscles tight as you lower it back down and then return it to the start position. Repeat this with the other leg (extend leg, lift leg, lower leg, return to start position). Your back should remain stationary throughout these movements. When you are

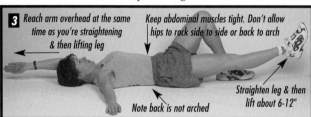

able to do this without difficulty you're ready to progress to the next level, shown in figure 3. In this more advanced stabilization exercise, you'll simultaneously reach one arm overhead and straighten the opposite leg while still maintaining constant tension in your abdominal muscles. Move slowly and rhythmically, alternating right arm / left leg with left arm / right leg.

KEY POINTS

1. The goal is to maintain constant tension in the abdominal muscles throughout the movement and to keep your spine stable in spite of the movement of your arms and legs.

2. Start with moving just your legs before you progress to moving diagonal pairs.

3. Repeat the movement for 10-30 repetitions, moving slowly and rhythmically.

Curl Ups

This exercise works the oblique abdominal muscles. Lie on your back with your hips and knees flexed 90 degrees. You may rest your feet on a chair, or simply hold them in the air as shown here. Place your left hand behind your head and extend your right arm out to the side. Tighten your abdominal muscles **before** you do any movement with your upper body. Hold your abdominal muscles tight, and lift and rotate your torso so that your left shoulder moves toward your right knee. Keep your right arm on the floor throughout the movement. The goal isn't to lift your body high off the floor; it is to isolate the abdominal muscles to perform the work.

If your neck muscles feel strained, try to relax the weight of your head into your hand and focus your attention on using your abdominal muscles to

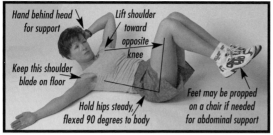

Hand behind head for support
Lift shoulder toward opposite knee
Keep this shoulder blade on floor
Hold hips steady, flexed 90 degrees to body
Feet may be propped on a chair if needed for abdominal support

lift your head and left shoulder toward your right knee. Move slowly and rhythmically, maintaining the "up" position for about 3 seconds. Remember to keep your abdominal muscles tight throughout the movement and try not to hold your breath. Perform all your repetitions one direction and then switch to put your other hand behind your head and lift to the opposite knee.

KEY POINTS

1. Keep your outstretched arm on the floor for support and to keep you from lifting your torso too high.

2. Tighten your abdominal muscles **before** you begin to lift your head and shoulder up off the floor.

3. Move slowly and rhythmically, holding the "up" position for about 3 seconds.

4. Don't hold your breath.

5. Make the motion rotational to insure firing of the oblique abdominal muscles. Lift the elbow toward the opposite knee.

Opposite Arm and Leg Raise

This exercise can be done over a chair, or for more challenge you can use one of the large, inflatable therapeutic balls. Lie face down across the seat of the chair, so that the chair does not rest directly under your chest.

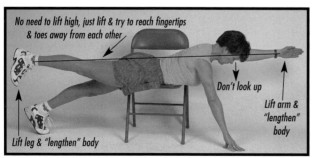

No need to lift high, just lift & try to reach fingertips & toes away from each other
Don't look up
Lift arm & "lengthen" body
Lift leg & "lengthen" body

Let your arms hang down so that your fingertips rest on the floor. Make sure to keep your head in neutral alignment, neither looking up nor allowing it to hang down. Your back should be perfectly flat and level. Maintain this alignment while you lift your opposite arm and leg. Your goal is to be able to lift the arm and leg to a position level with (but not above) your back. Initially you may not be able to attain this straight alignment, but with time and practice you should be able to. Make sure to maintain your back and neck in their neutral alignment as you lift the arm and leg; avoid the temptation to look up. Hold the "up" position for 2-3 seconds. If you have discomfort in your back when you do this, you're probably not maintaining your neutral spine position or you're trying to lift too high. Adjust your position, and try lifting the arm and leg only slightly off the floor. If you continue to have discomfort you're not ready to lift diagonal pairs; try lifting one arm at a time and then one leg at a time. Eventually you'll be able to lift diagonal pairs.

KEY POINTS

1. Maintain a neutral alignment of your back and neck throughout the exercise

2. Lift the arm and leg slowly; and <u>don't lift higher than your back.</u>

3. Hold the "up" position for about 2-3 seconds, and then repeat on the opposite side.

4. For additional challenge, use a large inflatable therapeutic ball in place of the chair. You'll be surprised how much more difficult the exercise is when you have to keep the ball from rolling around underneath you as you lift your arm and leg.

5. If you have discomfort with this, try lifting only one extremity at a time and pay close attention to spinal and neck alignment.

"Flying like a bird"

Lie face down across the seat of a chair, so that the chair does *not* rest directly underneath your chest. You can also do this one using a large,

Start here, hands resting on floor. Keep your back flat & eyes looking at the floor between your hands

Look here

inflatable therapeutic ball if you want a little more challenge. Let your arms hang down toward the floor and align your back and neck so that they are level and straight. You should maintain this neutral alignment throughout the exercise. Avoid the temptation to look up as you perform the movement. Lift your arms straight out to the side, as if you were flying like a bird. Maintain a small amount of bend in the elbow as you lift your arms. You should feel the muscles in your upper back working as you perform this exercise. Hold the "up" position for 2-3 seconds and move rhythmically and slowly through the exercise. If you feel discomfort in your lower back, you are probably not maintaining a neutral spine alignment. Recheck your position and try the

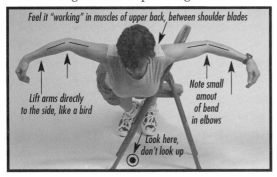

Feel it "working" in muscles of upper back, between shoulder blades

Lift arms directly to the side, like a bird

Note small amout of bend in elbows

Look here, don't look up

exercise again, but don't lift your arms quite as high. If you continue to have lower back discomfort, scoot back on the chair so that it partially supports your chest, thus alleviating some of the workload on the lower back muscles.

KEY POINTS

1. Maintain a neutral, level alignment of the spine and head throughout the exercise.

2. Move slowly and rhythmically through the exercise, holding the "up" position for 2-3 seconds.

3. Keep your elbows *slightly* bent throughout the movement.

4. If you have discomfort in your lower back, check your spine and head alignment to make sure you're maintaining a neutral position. You may need to scoot back on the chair to allow it to partially support your chest and reduce the load on the lower back muscles.

"Swim"

Lie face down across the seat of a chair, so that the chair does *not* rest directly beneath your chest. You can also do this one using a large, inflat-

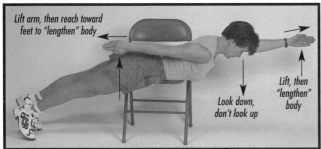

Lift arm, then reach toward feet to "lengthen" body

Look down, don't look up

Lift, then "lengthen" body

able therapeutic ball if you want a little more challenge. Maintain a neutral, straight spinal and head alignment throughout the exercise.

Start with your arms hanging straight down toward the floor. Alternately lift one arm forward and up over your head while you simultaneously lift the other one back toward your hips. This movement sort of resembles the position of your arms if you were swimming the crawl stroke...hence the name of the exercise. The emphasis should be on maximizing the distance between the fingertips of the left hand and those of the right, rather than trying to lift the arms high into the air. Hold the "up" position for 2-3 seconds, and then reverse directions. Keep your toes on the floor throughout the exercise; the only movement should be in your arms. If you have lower back discomfort when doing this, you may not be maintaining your neutral spinal alignment, or you may need to scoot back on the chair so that it supports a little bit of the weight of your chest. Move slowly and rhythmically through the movement, avoiding the temptation to "look up" when you reach overhead.

KEY POINTS

1. Maintain a neutral alignment of your back and neck as you lift your arms, avoid the temptation to "look up" as you reach overhead.

2. Rather than lifting your arms up high, focus on trying to maximize the distance between the fingertips of one hand and the fingertips of the other hand.

3. If you have discomfort in your lower back as you do this exercise, check to make sure you're maintaining a neutral alignment of your back and neck. You may need to scoot back on the chair so that the seat supports a little more of the weight of your chest.

"Superman"

Lie face down across the seat of a chair, so that the chair does *not* rest directly beneath your chest. You can also do this one using a large, inflatable therapeutic ball if you want a little more challenge. Make sure you maintain a neutral alignment of your back and neck throughout the exercise; avoid the temptation to "look up" as you reach your arms overhead. Start with your hands up near your shoulders. Keep your elbows pulled back so that your arms are in line with your body.

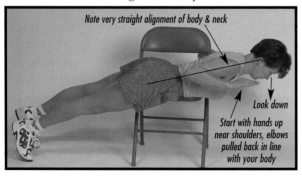

Note very straight alignment of body & neck

Look down

Start with hands up near shoulders, elbows pulled back in line with your body

Reach your arms overhead as far as you can, trying to keep them as high off the floor as you are able to. If your shoulders are tight, you may not be able to keep the arms in line with your body, but this will improve as your strength and range of motion increase. Hold the "reach" position for

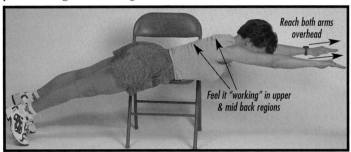

Reach both arms overhead

Feel it "working" in upper & mid back regions

2-3 seconds, and then return your arms to the start position. If you have lower back pain as you do this exercise, you may need to allow your arms to drop a little. It may also be helpful to scoot back a little on the chair so that it supports a little more of the weight of your chest.

KEY POINTS

1. Maintain neutral alignment of your back and neck throughout the movement; avoid the temptation to "look up" as you reach overhead.

2. Keep your elbows pulled up and back in the start position. Try to reach as high overhead as possible.

3. Hold the "reach" position for 2-3 seconds.

4. If you have lower back discomfort when you do this, allow your arms to be a little lower, and consider scooting back a little on the chair so that it supports the weight of your chest.

SUMMARY OF STRENGTH EXERCISES

Progressing your exercises is tricky business. If you jump the gun too soon and move to a more challenging exercise before your body is ready, you risk causing yourself an injury.

> It can't be emphasized enough – start conservatively and progress systematically and slowly through these exercises. If you are currently injured, you'd be well advised to check with your health care provider to see which (if any) of these exercises are appropriate for you.

Beginners:

- **Squats** – start with shallow depth, and then progress gradually to chair depth. Use body weight only.

- **Lunges** – start with forward and straight lateral lunges using short stride and shallow depth. Progress gradually to deeper depth and larger stride length. Use body weight only.

▪ **Abdominal stabilization progressions** – start with movement of single extremity (for example, just one arm at a time or just one leg at a time), and then gradually progress to moving diagonal pairs.

▪ **Back extensor strength** – start with the "opposite arm and leg lift" but lift only one extremity at a time. Gradually progress to lifting diagonal pairs (opposite arm and leg simultaneously).

Intermediates:

▪ **Squats** – squat to chair depth using body weight only or small hand weights for additional resistance.

▪ **Lunges** – In addition to forward and lateral lunges, also try the lateral rotation lunge. Stride length and depth should be moderate, with the use of body weight only or small hand weights for additional resistance

▪ **Back extensor strength** – start with "Fly", "Swim" and "Superman" exercises using a chair for support. Transition to lifting diagonal pairs on the "Opposite arm and leg lift" exercise.

▪ **Abdominal exercise** – begin with the diagonal curl ups. Continue progressing the abdominal stabilization exercises by moving arm and opposite leg simultaneously.

Advanced:

▪ **Squats** – progress to a depth where buttocks descend to knee height (but not lower), and incorporate the use of hand weights or barbells for added resistance. Highly advanced athletes may perform plyometric style squats such as jump squats or depth squats. Since these are very intense and carry with them a greater risk of injury they will not be covered in detail here. **Only the most advanced athletes, who have already established a substantial base of strength training, should perform plyometric style exercises.**

▪ **Lunges** – may be performed in all directions, using both a "lunge and return" as well as "progressive" or "walking lunge" style. Use a stride length and depth of lunge that offers maximum challenge. Hand weights or barbells can be used to provide additional resistance. Using a rubberized tether cord around the hips to provide resistance from different angles can introduce a substantial element of challenge. Holding a weighted medicine ball and incorporating upper body movements with the lunges can emphasize core strength.

- **Balance and Reach exercises** – These should only be performed when the athlete is able to accomplish squats and lunges without difficulty or pain. The balance and reach exercises can be introduced before full squat depth or lunge distance is attained, **if** the athlete is conservative in their approach and utilizes "legal cheating" such as using a wall or chair for balance assistance. Generally speaking, the balance and reach exercises are the most challenging of those presented here; so a conservative approach is the best way. Depending on the athlete's particular strengths and weaknesses, different balance and reach exercises will be relatively easier or harder. It is best to consult a skilled coach, exercise physiologist or physical therapist if you are recovering from an injury and are having difficulty with progressing to balance and reach exercises.

- **Abdominal stabilization progression** – Use of VERY light handheld weights or cuff weights around the ankle can provide a level of challenge for the most advanced athletes. This should only be done if the athlete is able to perform at least 30 repetitions of the exercise (unweighted) without difficulty.

- **Diagonal curl ups** – Use of a lightweight medicine ball can offer additional resistance on this exercise. It is important to realize that good form must be maintained when additional resistance is provided.

- **Back extensor strengthening** – Use of a therapeutic ball to challenge balance while performing the exercises will add a bit of difficulty. Holding small dumbbells or using cuff weights may provide additional resistance. Start with a very light weight (1 lb.) and progress systematically. A reasonable target for the exercises presented would be to perform 30 repetitions while holding 3-5 pound weights.

REFERENCES CHAPTER FOUR

1. Adams K, O'Shea P, O'Shea KL. *Aging: Its effects on strength, power, flexibility, and bone density.* Strength and Cond Journal, Vol.21, No. 2, pp. 65-77, 1999.

2. Burr DB. *Bone, Exercise and Stress Fractures.* Exercise and Sports Sciences Reviews, Vol. 25 pp. 171-194, 1997.

3. Dressenforfer RH, Wade CE, Claybaugh J, Cucinell SA, Timmis GC. *Effects of 7 successive days of unaccustomed prolonged exercise on aerobic performance and tissue damage in fitness joggers.* Int. J. Sports Med. 12:55-61, 1991.

4. Gray G. *Lower Extremity Functional Profile.* Wynn Marketing, 1995.

CHAPTER FIVE

TRAINING ERRORS

Entire books on training have been written, and the reader is encouraged to check the bibliography at the end of this chapter for a few excellent texts that go into great detail about training for different distances and events. This chapter will focus on the very basic parameters of training with an emphasis on the most common training errors committed by athletes in their pursuit of excellence.

> ◑ *Training to improve fitness or to improve performance involves placing stress on the body and there is a fine line between enough stress to stimulate an improvement and too much stress, leading to injury. It is no surprise that some researchers report that approximately 33% of serious runners are injured in any given year[2].*

As noted in the previous chapters, training errors are a consistent factor in the onset of most injuries. Training errors are nearly universally cited as a primary causative factor in most running injuries and in fact have been reported to account for two thirds of injuries[2]. In one study of 155 British triathletes, overuse was the reported cause of 41% of the injuries, and two thirds of those injuries were attributed to running[3]. Clearly training can take a toll on you, but armed with a basic understanding of how the body adapts you can avoid many of the more common mistakes.

System Adaptation

When first beginning a running or walking program, shortness of breath will often be the limiting factor. The cardiovascular system, which delivers oxygenated blood to all areas of the body including working muscles, is crucial in successful performance. Thankfully this system adapts relatively quickly to the regular imposition of stress afforded by a systematic training program. Within a matter of a few short weeks, most individuals with moderate levels of fitness are able to run continuously without "running out of wind". This readily apparent adaptation may lead the new athlete to believe that he or she is ready to increase the training load. However, other tissues in the body may not be as far along in the adaptation process and therein lays the problem. Not all tissues adapt to stress at the same rate. For instance, in a previous chapter stress fractures were mentioned as one of the more common injuries incurred by beginning athletes. The primary reason for this is the way bone adapts to stress through "remodeling". As with any remodel, there's a "demolition" phase before construction can begin. In the case of bone, that phase is known as bone resorption and then the formation of new bone follows. If the stress on the bony tissue is such that bone resorption outpaces bone formation, significant weakening of the bony tissue may result. Continuing to train on this now weakened tissue will often lead to injury. **While cardiovascular adaptation may take only a few weeks, muscular, ligamentous and bony tissue often require several weeks to several months of systematic training to adapt and attain optimum strength. It is no surprise that most injuries occur in these slower adapting tissues.**

Training Parameters

The four basic parameters of training that can be easily manipulated include distance (or duration), speed (or intensity), terrain (hills, trails etc.) and frequency (days per week). It seems obvious, but needs to be stated – **a sharp increase in any of these parameters carries with it a substantial increase in the risk of injury.** In short, slow and systematic changes in your training will be your best route to success. By systematically varying your training from day to day and week to week you can optimize your body's ability to adapt to training. This systematic progression and variation of training is called "periodization" and implies that different aspects of training may be emphasized at different times. For example, building a base of mileage is usually necessary before beginning to focus on speed. Problems may arise when the athlete attempts to increase more than one parameter at a time. For example if an athlete simultaneously adds significant mileage *and* speed to his weekly workload, this may overload the body's ability to adapt and an injury may result. A good general rule of thumb for most adult athletes is to **build endurance (distance) first, then speed.** The second rule of thumb is to manipulate only one parameter at a time (distance, speed, hills, frequency, terrain).

Establishing a foundation

The initial phase or period of training is referred to as base building and may comprise many weeks or even months of training for a beginning athlete depending on their initial fitness level. Even for the seasoned athlete, each year should have a period of training that focuses on base building and injury prevention before the transition into a racing season.

This phase is devoted not only to building a base of mileage, but also to strength training and flexibility exercises to prevent injury. The emphasis

➲ *Easy pace is defined as a pace that is comfortable; one at which you may easily carry on a conversation with a training partner. For athletes who have some racing experience, this may correlate to 70-80% of your 5K or 10K race pace.*

during this phase is on easy paced runs. Easy pace is defined as a pace that is comfortable; one at which you may easily carry on a conversation with a training partner. For athletes who have some racing experience, this may correlate to 70-80% of your 5K or 10K race pace. Perhaps now is the time to point out that one of the most consistent and most often overlooked training errors committed by "experienced" athletes is simply going out the door too close to target race pace every run. In other words, they've lost touch with the concept of "easy pace". **Establishing a foundation of mileage and learning to run "easy" are two very important concepts to learn.**

Building distance first

By varying the duration or distance from day to day, the body is allowed adequate time to respond to the stress of training. Most athletes will be able to build endurance effectively by doing one relatively longer workout each week, filling the other days with alternating medium and shorter distances. For example:

Sun	Mon.	Tues.	Wed.	Thurs.	Fri.	Sat·	Total mileage
8	2	2	4	2	4	2	24 miles per week

In this example, the "long" day is Sunday and represents about 33% of the weekly mileage. "Easy" days are Monday, Tuesday, Thursday and Saturday. "Medium" days are Wednesday and Friday. For the athlete who would prefer to train 5 days per week rather than 7, the following may be an option:

Sun	Mon.	Tues.	Wed.	Thurs.	Fri.	Sat.	Total mileage
8	off	3	5	3	5	off	24 miles per week

Training is by nature dependent on many personal variables including the time available each day to train, personal preferences, and family and job commitments. Each athlete will inevitably find a pattern that works best for them, however following a "hard-easy" schedule such as the one presented here allows for recovery and adaptation. Some athletes may feel it is "hardly worth lacing my shoes" for a training day as short as 2 miles, but many researchers feel that the increased blood flow that comes from running those "short" days may actually enhance recovery. Never underestimate the value of REST. Rest can be in the form of a day off, or a short day, or a cross training day. Rest days are vital to allow the body time to recover.

Increases in mileage should be made gradually. A generally accepted rule of thumb is to increase mileage by no more than 10% per week. Beginning athletes or those who are returning from an injury may find it is better to increase mileage only every other week or every third week. Once a stable base of mileage has been established, the athlete may begin to focus on other aspects of training such as hills, terrain challenges (trails) or speed work. Even the seasoned athlete should spend a bare minimum of 4-6 weeks in the base building phase each year before moving on. The beginning athlete may spend 6 months or more in this phase before transitioning to more intense training.

The following would be a reasonable 10-week progression for a beginning athlete of average fitness. Note that the mileage is first added to the "long" day – with the intention of building endurance first. Next the "medium" days are lengthened, and finally mileage is added to the "short" days. Recovery is allowed by alternating relatively longer and shorter days. Total mileage per week is increased by about 10% per week.

	Sun.	Mon.	Tues.	Wed.	Thurs.	Fri.	Sat.	Total Mileage
Week 1	3	Off	1.5	2	1.5	2	Off	10
Week 2	4	0	1.5	2	1.5	2	0	11
Week 3	4	0	1.5	2.5	1.5	2.5	0	12
Week 4	5	0	1.5	2.5	1.5	2.5	0	13
Week 5	5	0	1.5	3	1.5	3	0	14
Week 6	6	0	1.75	3	1.75	3	0	15.5
Week 7	6.5	0	2	3	2	3	0	16.5
Week 8	7	0	2	3	2	4	0	18
Week 9	7.5	0	2	4	2	4	0	19.5
Week 10	8	0	2	4	2	4	0	20

Ready for a challenge?

Hill running represents one form of more intense training and is an excellent way to build strength when done properly. Excessive emphasis on hill running however will increase the risk of injury. As in most aspects of training, more is not necessarily better. Most injuries that occur in conjunction with hill training can be associated with the downhill portion. Running or walking downhill causes a marked increase in ground reaction forces and consequently an increased load on the muscles. Moderation is the key to success when using hills to improve your strength. Work on gentle to moderate inclines rather than steep hills. Begin by adding a few short rolling hills to your training regimen, and avoid the tendency to "race" down

> *Keep the hill work to no more than 10% of your weekly mileage initially, and even seasoned athletes would do well to avoid training on extremely hilly courses on a daily basis.*

the hill. Work on maintaining even effort going up the hill and landing lightly on your feet when going down the hill. Athletes who train on treadmills are sometimes tempted to keep the treadmill elevated on an incline throughout their workout. This is a particularly bad idea, as the chronic uphill terrain can contribute to loss of flexibility in the leg muscles, and increased strain on the lower back. When training on a treadmill, use the incline judiciously; hills of 2-6% for 1-3 minutes duration are a reasonable challenge for most athletes who are unaccustomed to training on hills. You probably would not pick a continuous uphill course if you were training outdoors, and there's no need to do so on a treadmill either!

Changing pace

Another way to increase the intensity of your training is to focus on increasing your speed. Speed based training can take the form of short bursts of 30 seconds to 3 minutes at 5K race pace, or longer continuous bouts of 15-20 minutes at 85% of 5K race pace or even longer stretches at 10K or marathon race pace. The length and speed of the sessions will be dependent on the event you're training for. By nature shorter races like the 3K or 5K races will require somewhat faster speedwork than longer races like a marathon or half marathon. **Excessive emphasis on speed work is probably one of the most common errors committed by experienced athletes.** When reviewing the training logs of injured athletes I quite often find that nearly every run is done at 90% or more of target race pace. This is quite clearly a recipe for injury. Jack Daniels, a respected coach, exercise physiologist, and author, breaks speed work down into several different types including "threshold", "intervals", and "repetition" paces. Each type of speedwork is emphasized at different points in train-ing and is used judiciously. He recommends doing no more than 10% of your weekly mileage at threshold pace, 8% at interval pace and only 5% at repetition pace[1]. Even without knowing the specifics of those paces, it is clear to see that training at faster paces should comprise no more than about 20% of your total weekly mileage. When doing the faster intervals (at 5K race pace or faster) it is important to allow adequate recovery between intervals. A good general rule of thumb is to allow a recovery period roughly equal in duration to the work bout. In other words if you are doing 800 meter repeats at 5K race pace and each interval takes about 2:30 to accomplish, then you need to allow 2:30 for recovery in between each interval.

Mix it up!

With these parameters in mind, it becomes clear that not only should the athlete vary the distance covered from day to day they should also carefully incorporate rest days, hill training, and speedwork to their weekly training. For example, the following week incorporates a long workout for endurance building, several easy workouts for recovery, and two relatively more intense workouts in the form of hills and/or speedwork.

Sun.	Mon.	Tues.	Wed.	Thurs.	Fri.	Sat.	Total
16	4	4	8	4	8	Off	44
Long run at Easy pace	Easy pace	Easy pace	Incorporate 4-5 miles of hilly terrain **or** threshold pace running	Easy pace	4-6 miles of speed work	Rest	

It should be emphasized that the training weeks presented here are for demonstration only – each athlete has distinct needs and goals that will help determine the ideal program for them. In this regard an experi-enced coach may be your best investment.

Coming back from an injury

Once an athlete has sustained an injury, returning to their previous activity is often at the forefront of their thoughts. This period of injury rehabilitation should be an ideal time to look back through the training log and search for training errors such as adding mileage too quickly or training at too fast a pace. Careful documentation of training can provide

◗ *Careful documentation of training can provide a wealth of information to the athlete, coach and any medical professionals who are consulted in the rehabilitation process.*

a wealth of information to the athlete, coach and any medical professionals who are consulted in the rehabilitation process. A thorough training log will include not only the distance (or duration) of the training bout but also the terrain, the speed, and any environmental factors that were significant like heat, rain, cold, etc. Comments about the way you felt during or after the workout may later be reviewed and reveal important clues about the genesis of any injuries. Make note of the date that shoes were purchased, and keep track of the mileage on them. Once errors are identified then adjustments to the training plan can be made.

The return to training can begin once an injury is well on its way to resolution. For some injuries a day or two off will be plenty, others may take several weeks or even months. Pain is your body's way of signaling you that something isn't right. Continuing to train in spite of pain is generally not a good idea, and will most likely prolong your injury.

When in doubt, a few days of rest is usually the best choice. Use the following checklist to determine if you're ready to resume training.

⊚ There should be no pain at rest.

⊚ There should be no discomfort with normal activities of daily living including walking, moving from sit to stand, and ascending or descending stairs.

⊚ Any swelling that was present previously should be resolved or minimal.

⊚ Any tenderness to the touch that was present previously should be resolved.

⊚ If activity was restricted by a physician (i.e. because of a stress fracture), follow up has been completed and clearance to resume activities given.

How long will this take?

How quickly one is able to return to the previous level of training depends in large part on the length of time that training was interrupted. One rule of thumb is that the amount of time devoted to returning to the previous level of activity should be equal to the amount of time that training was interrupted. In other words if a training break of 6 weeks was necessary due to a stress fracture, a period of about six weeks will be necessary to return to the previous level of training. A short break of a few days may entail only a minor adjustment in the form of elimination of the more intense workouts for the week and a focus on only easy paced training. Longer duration breaks of several months may mean that training is resumed in the form of walking and intermittent jogging, with a gradual resumption of continuous jogging and eventual increase in mileage. This general rule of thumb is by no means precise, and the athlete should not feel defeated if they take a little longer than expected to resume training. It is this period of resumption of training that often traps athletes who are over-eager to return to their previous routine. The training errors, which were influential in the onset of the original injury, must be adequately addressed and corrected; and training must progress at such a pace as to avoid another injury. The rules of thumb for adding mileage and intensity apply here as well as when beginning a running or walking program.

> ❯ *The training errors, which were influential in the onset of the original injury, must be adequately addressed and corrected; and training must progress at such a pace as to avoid another injury.*

Cross training

Cross training during rehabilitation of an injury is an option for some. **It is important to check with your medical professional or an experienced coach regarding any limitations or restrictions on your activity before pursuing a program of alternate activities.** Each injury has specific biomechanical characteristics and without proper guidance you may choose an activity that actually makes your condition worse rather than allowing for healing. For some athletes, deep water running or swimming can enable them to maintain cardiorespiratory conditioning while rehabilitating an injury. Others may find that stationary cycling or use of low-impact cardiovascular equipment such as cross-country ski simulators, stair climbers, or an elliptical trainer offers an alternative avenue for training. No matter what type of cross training you choose to use, it is important to listen to your body and insure that the activity does not cause symptoms. For many athletes, the method of cross training they choose introduces a new type of stress to the body and should be introduced gradually in order to avoid the soreness that comes when you start something new. Cross training may help to minimize the loss of cardiorespiratory conditioning that accompanies a long training break but it is important to realize that the actions involved in these alternative forms of training are not identical to running or walking. So, no matter how well you've maintained your cardiorespiratory fitness through cross training, you must resume training slowly and systematically to allow the musculoskeletal system adequate time to re-adapt to the specific demands of running or walking.

How quickly can I come back?

Guidelines for resumption of training are difficult to generalize, as specific injuries will call for specific adjustments in training. Additionally, individual differences in fitness level prior to the injury may affect the rate at which activity may be resumed. When trying to determine how much you should do, it is better to err on the side of too little rather than too much. Do less than you think you are capable of and when in doubt, make your transition more gradual than you think you need to. Obviously the best course is to consult with a reputable coach or sports medicine professional to assist you in this transition from rehabilitating an injury to returning to training. A sensible approach would be to resume training at 50% of your previous mileage if you've been off more than 2 weeks or 30% of your previous mileage if you've been off more than 4 weeks. An interruption of training that lasts more than 8 weeks will necessitate a very gradual resumption of training and for some may require "starting all over again". When resuming training, runs should be at easy pace, and hills and specific speedwork avoided until at least 75% of the weekly mileage prior to injury has been achieved. The following should serve as general guidelines both to those starting a training program and those resuming training after an injury.

> ● *When trying to determine how much you should do, it is better to err on the side of too little rather than too much. Do less than you think you are capable of and when in doubt, make your transition more gradual than you think you need to.*

- ◻ Build distance (endurance) first, and then speed.
- ◻ Add mileage gradually, increasing total weekly mileage by no more than 10% per week.
- ◻ When hill training or speedwork are added to the training, do so gradually. Specific speed work in the form of threshold (tempo), interval, or repetition training should comprise no more than about 20% of your weekly total mileage.
- ◻ Monitor your body's response to training by keeping a detailed log. This information will serve you well when injuries occur and will hold clues as to how you can avoid them in the future.
- ◻ When returning from an injury, resume training at a reduced pace and

reduced total mileage per week. The transition to your previous level of training will take about the same amount of time as your break from training.

◘ Seek the advice of a reputable coach or sports medicine professional to help you maximize your training without bringing on further injury or impeding the healing of current injuries.

REFERENCES CHAPTER FIVE

1. James SL. *Running injuries to the knee.* J Am. Acad. Orthop. Surg. Nov; 3(6):309-318, 1995.

2. Korkia PK, Tunstall-Pedoe DS, Maffulli N. *An epidemiological investigation of training and injury patterns in British triathletes.* Br. J. Sports Med. 3.Sep;28(3):191-196, 1994.

4. Daniels JD. *Daniels' Running Formula.* Human Kinetics Publishers, Champaign IL, 1998.

BIBLIOGRAPHY

1. Daniels JD. *Daniels' Running Formula.* Human Kinetics Publishers, Champaign IL, 1998.

2. Finke W, Finke P. *Marathoning Start to Finish, 2nd Edition.* W'Yeast Publications, 2000.

3. Fixx J. *The complete book of running.* Random House, 1977.

4. Galloway J. *Galloway's Book on Running.* Shelter Publications, 1994.

5. Galloway J. *Marathon!* Phidippides Publications, 2000.

6. Henderson J. *Marathon Training: the Proven 100-Day Program for Success.* Human Kinetics Publishers, 1997.

7. Lydiard A. *Running to the Top.* Meyer & Meyer Fachverlag und Buchhandel GmbH, 1997.

8. Martin DE, Coe PN. *Better Training for Distance Runners.* Human Kinetics Publishers, Champaign IL, 1997.

9. Noakes TD, Noakes T. *The Lore of Running.* Human Kinetics Publishers, Champaign IL, 1991.

10. Sheehan GA. *Running and Being: The total experience.* Second Wind, 1998.

EPILOGUE

KEEPING IT IN PERSPECTIVE

Injuries to athletes are unfortunately pretty common, and many, if not most, can be avoided with a little attention to some simple details as outlined in the previous chapters. Life is a delicate balancing act, and each aspect of life (job, emotional stress, physical stress, etc.) has an impact on the other aspects. "Keeping it in perspective" means that when an injury occurs and you're forced to take a break from the sport you love, try to realize that it is only one aspect of who you are as a person. You are more than "an athlete". You are a complex individual with many facets to your life...one of which is your love of your sport. Obsessing about your injury will not win you friends, nor will it speed your healing process. Take the necessary steps to enhance the environment for healing – rest, adequate nutrition, and adequate hydration all help. Patience is a must as your body performs the miracle of healing. Cross training is an option for some and may help to alleviate the anxiety that comes when you're not able to run or train like you want to. **Preventing injuries is the primary goal, and a more informed athlete can make the important decisions and adjustments to training that can help fend off injuries.** Once injured, an informed athlete has a better plan for how to treat the injury and return to activity as quickly as possible. It is hoped that the information provided here will help to point you in the right direction.

The information provided in the previous chapters is only an overview of a broad scope of material from the rapidly evolving field of exercise science. "Keeping it in perspective" also means that as new information comes to light, old "truths" may well be found to be nothing more than folklore and myth. It is important to realize that the field of exercise science is still in a relative infancy. The best coaches and medical professionals will stay up to date and be a good sounding board when you find you've run into the proverbial brick wall in your training.

May you always have the wind at your back and run strong and injury-free for years to come.

ACKNOWLEDGEMENTS

I'd like to take this opportunity to thank some wonderful people who were instrumental not only in the publication of this book but also in many other aspects of my life both as an athlete and a professional.

Kelly Reed, PT – thanks for being the model for all the exercises (less than five months after having a baby!) Thanks too for the moral support along the way, and for being a sounding board and brilliant clinician. I learned more from you in the time we worked together than you'll ever know.

Patti and Warren Finke – thanks for introducing me to the joys of marathoning, and for sharing your love of Oregon with me. Thanks for getting me started in coaching. You introduced me to the unique joys of a great mud run in Forest Park, followed by a big stack of pancakes and steaming hot coffee.

My family – thanks for the encouragement along the way.

A very special thanks to my husband and best friend Bob, whose unfailing belief in me has carried me through thick and thin for more years than I care to count. Running alongside you has brought me more joy than you know. And last but not least, thanks to Bear and Sunny, who put up with their share of missed walks and runs as I tried to finish this project.

GLOSSARY

Abduction – the lateral movement of the limbs away from the midline of the body.

Adduction – the movement of the limbs toward the midline of the body.

Anterior – Before or in front of. Anatomically, toward the front of the body.

Atrophy – a wasting or reduction in size of a structure.

Biomechanics – the science of action of mechanical forces on living organisms. Includes forces which arise from within and outside the body.

Bunion – Inflammation and thickening of the bursa of the joint of the great toe, usually associated with marked enlargement of the joint and displacement of the toe laterally.

Bursa – A padlike sac or cavity found in connecting tissue usually in the vicinity of joints. It is lined with synovial membrane and contains a fluid, synovia, which acts to reduce friction between tendon and bone, tendon and ligament, or between other structures where friction is likely to occur.

Bursitis – Inflammation of a bursa, especially those located between bony prominences and muscle or tendon as the shoulder and knee.

Calcaneus – the heel bone.

Concentric contraction – a muscular contraction which involves a shortening of the muscle, for example when a weight is lifted against gravity or when one comes to a standing position from a seated position.

Connective tissue – Tissue which supports and connects other tissues and tissues and parts. Connective tissues are highly vascular with the exception of cartilage.

Eccentric contraction – a muscular contraction in which the muscle is gradually lengthened. For example, when a weight is slowly lowered or when one lowers oneself into a chair.

Extension – the act of straightening a joint.

Femur – the thigh bone. It extends from the hip to the knee and is the longest and strongest bone in the body.

Flexion – the act of bending a joint.

Gait – manner of walking.

Gait cycle – the interval of time from heel strike on one side through the entire weight bearing phase and swing phase until that heel contacts the ground again.

Hypermobility – from the Greek root word "hyper" meaning above, excessive or beyond. A condition in which the motion at a joint or series of joints is greater than normal.

Hypomobility – from the Greek root word "hypo" meaning under. A condition in which the motion of a joint or series of joints is less than normal.

Kinetic chain – a term used to refer to the intricate linkage of the segments of the body, indicating that motion at one segment is translated to segments above and below. For example, in a standing position, pronation of the foot is translated to internal rotation of the tibia and femur.

Lateral – to the side. In anatomical reference, away from the midline

Lesion – an injury or wound.

Ligament – A band or sheet of strong fibrous connective tissue that connects bone to bone and serves to facilitate or limit motion.

Medial – toward the middle. In anatomical reference, toward the midline of the body.

Metatarsalgia – Severe pain or cramp in the anterior portion of the metatarsus (forefoot).

Modality – A method of application or the employment of any therapeutic agent.

Orthotics – from the Greek root word "ortho", meaning straight. Orthotics or orthoses are devices used to correct, straighten or compensate for a structural deformity.

Periodization – the systematic alteration of training over a period of weeks or months, or the variation in training during a week.

Periostitis – an inflammation of the membrane covering the bone, known as the periosteum.

Peritendinitis – an inflammatory condition of the sheath of a tendon.

Pes cavus – a condition in which the arch contour is unusually high. Often, but not always accompanied by a hypomobility of the joints of the foot.

Pes planus – a condition in which the arch contour is unusually low. Often, but not always accompanied by a hypermobility of the joints of the foot.

Plantar Fascitis (also spelled fasciitis) – an inflammation of the plantar fascia.

Posterior – Toward the rear or back. Anatomically, toward the back of the body.

Pronation – a combined motion of the foot in the direction of eversion, dorsiflexion and abduction. The resultant motion in weight bearing is a relative collapsing of contour of the medial arch of the foot.

Proprioception – the awareness of posture, movement, and changes in equilibrium and the knowledge of position, weight and resistance of objects in relation to the body.

Supination – a combined motion of the foot in the direction of inversion, plantarflexion and adduction. The resultant motion in weight bearing is a relative elevation of the contour of the medial arch of the foot.

Synovial membrane – membrane lining the capsule of a joint. Produces synovia which is a colorless lubricating fluid of joints, bursae and tendon sheaths.

Synovitis – inflammation of a synovial membrane.

Tendinitis – (tendonitis) – from the Greek root word "itis" meaning inflammation. An inflammation of a tendon.

Tendon – Fibrous connective tissue that attaches muscle to bone.

Tenosynovitis (tendosynovitis) – Inflammation of a sheath of a tendon.

Tibia – the inner and larger bone of the lower leg between the knee and ankle.

Viscosity – State of being sticky or gummy.

Note most definitions taken from Taber's Cyclopedic Medical Dictionary, 13th Ed., F A Davis Co., 1977.

INDEX

TRAINING NOTES